Olga White

DOING
BUSINESS
IN THE
USSR

GW00393301

DOING BUSINESS IN THE USSR

Nicholas Louis   Alexander Mamut
Richard Charkham   Andrew Warren

KOGAN
PAGE

© Nicholas Louis, Alexander Mamut, Richard Charkham, Andrew Warren 1990
All rights reserved. No reproduction, copy, or transmission of this publication may be made without written permission.

No paragraph of this publication may be reproduced, copied or transmitted save with written permission or in accordance with the provisions of the Copyright Act 1956 (as amended), or under the terms of any licence permitting limited copying issued by the Copyright Licensing Agency, 33–34 Alfred Place, London WC1E 7DP.

Any person who does any unauthorised act in relation to this publication may be liable to criminal prosecution and civil claims for damages.

First published in 1990 by
Kogan Page Ltd,
120 Pentonville Rd, London N1 9JN

Typeset by BookEns, Saffron Walden, Essex

Printed and bound in Great Britain by Biddles Ltd, Guildford and Kings Lynn

British Library Cataloguing in Publication Data

A CIP catalogue record for this book is available from the British Library.

ISBN 0-7494-0222-9

Contents

The Authors

Nicholas Louis has an M.Phil in International Relations from Balliol College, Oxford, and works as a business consultant to western companies trading with the USSR.

Alexander Mamut has an MA in Law from Moscow University and works as a legal adviser on joint ventures to state and cooperative organisations in the USSR.

Richard Charkham is an English solicitor, a member of the Israel bar and is a partner in the firm of Rotlevy, Charkham, Segal & Co., advocates of Tel Aviv. He has served as counsel to a large international trading and finance group specialising in joint ventures.

Andrew Warren is a practising solicitor and a partner in the law firm, Talbot Creggy and Co.

Introduction

According to a well-known Russian anecdote a young soldier was standing guard outside the Winter Palace in Saint Petersburg in 1917 after the Russian revolution, his face displaying a discernible grin. An elderly lady approached him and, on seeing the smile, asked, 'Why are you looking so happy, young man?'

'Why? Because we're making sure there'll be no more rich people!'

The old lady retorted, 'But I thought you were supposed to make sure that there were going to be no more poor people!'

The irony of the above story is a true and sad reflection of the state of the mass of people in the Soviet Union today. There is a strong, pervasive feeling that the events of 1917, and the sacrifices suffered in the name of 'progress' since then, have been in vain.

It is difficult to describe the enormity of the task facing the Soviet Union's political leaders today. Fortunately it is not the function of this book to do so; but it is equally difficult to separate a discussion of recent business changes in the USSR from the political upheaval (a less dramatic word would be inappropriate) now taking place in the vast far flung country. We hope, therefore, that the reader will excuse our occasional forays into the political or quasi political area.

Although the business laws discussed in this book have been legislated with the dual objectives of providing a foundation for the introduction of free enterprise and encouraging western investment, they have been tacked on to a basically incompatible system. Indeed, opponents to the left of the present Soviet leadership, such as Democratic Russia, have demanded much faster and more far-reaching changes. Even so, the innovations we will discuss are certainly 'revolutionary', if viewed in the light of the system that had prevailed from the early years of communist rule, since when the very idea of personal initiative had been scorned.

The fact of the matter is that the developments that have taken place, for example, since the inception of the Law on

Cooperation in 1988 have been quite dramatic. By the end of 1989, 5.5 million people were employed by cooperatives, over 90 per cent of which had been formed over the previous 18 months. This may not sound much out of a population of over 290 million, but if the annual growth rate were to continue at only a half of the 300 per cent achieved in 1989 it would not be many years before most of the working population would be engaged in the activities of cooperative organisations.

The expression 'cooperative' should not be confused with the western conception of the word which is defined, for example, by the Longman Dictionary of Contemporary English (Harlow, 1987) as:

> firm, farm, shop etc. especially one that is owned by all the people who work in it . . .

The Soviet conception of the cooperative under the Law on Cooperation is more akin (although not entirely similar) to a private company, but its members (except those of consumer co-operatives) do not yet enjoy the privilege of limited liability.

As to joint ventures with foreign investors, the number registered on 31 October 1989 was 940. Compared to the figures for cooperatives the number of these operations, which are not all active, is still minimal. However, because this is the major channel available to foreigners for investment in the Soviet Union (in theory a foreigner could become a member of a cooperative and, under the very latest Law on Property, a foreign citizen or company may actually acquire property in the Soviet Union in his, her or its name), we have dedicated over one third of the book to this subject.

It had, in fact, been our original intention to devote an entire work to the subject of joint ventures. As we prepared the material, however, it became increasingly clear that a discussion on that subject could not be divorced from a general description of the profound changes that have been introduced by the legislative bodies of the Soviet Union over the past two or three years.

After reaching that decision, however, we began to question the wisdom of it, because it seemed that every day, before the ink was dry, another new law had been introduced. A stage was reached when we were seriously considering holding a demonstration outside the Kremlin pleading for no more laws to be passed until long after publication of the book! The hardest decision facing us, and the publishers, was when to publish. Eventually we decided on a particular date, resolving to add a stop press chapter to cover any important changes introduced prior to final printing. One rumour, however, that was aired very late for us is, if it materialises, likely to prove the most drastic reform of all. This is that the State planning authority, *Gosplan*, and the State 'wholesaler', *Gossnab* (about which you will read in the opening chapter), are to be dismantled in the not too distant future. Such a step would lead, in the absence of some similar set-up, to a real opening up of the Soviet economy to free market influences.

We have divided the book into four main parts. The first deals with the general background matters covering geographical, demographic, political, constitutional, economic, legal and bureaucratic aspects of the Soviet Union. This hors d'oeuvre is followed by a description of the new cooperative system, which has proved to be a very dynamic factor in the new era. Most of the remainder of the book is dedicated to joint ventures including a typical joint venture agreement which, we hope, will be of assistance to all those who enter into negotiations with a view to investing in the USSR by means of such a vehicle. For desert we have offered a general hints and guidance section covering such aspects as how to go about conducting negotiations and where *not* to eat. We would not presume to usurp the role of the several excellent guide books available on the Soviet Union such as 'The Complete Guide To The Soviet Union', published by Michael Joseph and St. Martin's Press, 'The Traveller's Survival Kit – The Soviet Union and Eastern Europe' published by Vacation Work and 'Louis' Motorist's Guide To The Soviet Union' published by Pergamon Press.

The reader may also be able to glean some information on how to fare in the Soviet Union from the many new specialist periodicals that are sprouting up. Many companies and banks have well established offices in Moscow and will be only too pleased to enlist new clients. The services of an experienced agent may well be needed to help the businessperson find his or her way through the language and cultural differences to be found in a country that is still not completely open to the outside world. We have attempted to provide the readers with enough background information to enable them to find their feet when embarking on business ventures in the Soviet Union.

We hope too that the person well versed in the intricacies of doing business there will find something of interest in this book, particularly in the coverage of the latest developments. Special attention has, for example, been given to the changes in Soviet legislation affecting international trade and which are intended to encourage an extension of the trade between this huge, largely untapped, market and the rest of the world.

Finally, we wish to thank Sarah whose acumen on the word processor is unrivalled, and Lucy whose endless cups of tea sustained us while the snow was falling outside.

London and Moscow,
April 1990

1
The geography and demography of the Soviet Union and the Soviet systems

In order to contemplate entering into a serious business venture in a strange country it is vital to have some knowledge of its geography and demography and of the political, economic and legal systems and conditions under which the business will operate. Nowhere is this pardonable banality more applicable than in the Union of Soviet Socialist Republics which will be referred to simply as the Soviet Union or the USSR.

No reader will have to be told that the Soviet Union, under the leadership of President Mikhail Sergeivitch Gorbachev, has embarked upon a period of drastic and rapid change. The object of this chapter is to set out the situation as at the time of going to press while, at the same time, demonstrating the most important changes that have occurred over the past five years. We will divide the discussion in this chapter into the geographical and demographic, political (constitutional), economic, banking and legal spheres and, inevitably, the bureaucracy.

Geography and demography

The Soviet Union is the largest country in the world, covering a total area of 22,402,200 sq km (8,649,489 sq mi) or about 14 per cent of the earth's land surface (it is more than twice the size of the next largest country, Canada) and its population of over 290,000,000 ranks third after the People's Republic of China, and India. The common error of referring to the USSR as Russia arises not only for historical reasons (the USSR is in some ways the successor to the Russian empire of the czars) but also from the fact that the Russians are the most dominant of its more than 120 nationalities and that their language is both the official one and the most widespread of the 200 or so spoken in the country.

With regard to natural resources, it might be easier to list those that are not available in the Soviet Union. The country is extremely well endowed with gold, oil, coal, iron, magnesium, copper, chrome, nickel, lead, potash, tin, zinc, platinum, diamonds, tungsten and aluminium. It is the world's number one producer of timber and its fishing industry is extensive. The major crops of the USSR are wheat, rye and other grains, tea, tobacco and cotton. It also produces dairy products, sugar beet and meat.

The USSR is divided into different areas and regions for various purposes. At the highest level there is a political-administrative division into 15 Soviet Socialist Republics normally referred to as 'union republics'. The largest of these is the Russian Soviet Federated Socialist Republic (RSFSR) which covers more than three quarters of the land area of the USSR and is the home of over half the country's population. The next largest, in terms of population, is the Ukrainian SSR with about 18 per cent of the total populace, while the Kazakh SSR (Kazakhstan) is physically the next largest, covering 12 per cent of the total land area. In fact, in area, the Kazakhstan is larger than all the other republics put together (except for Russia). The 13 union republics after Russia and Ukraine (in diminishing population size) are: Uzbekistan, Kazakhstan, Byelorussia (or White Russia), Azerbaidzhan, Georgia, Tadzhikistan, Moldavia, Kirgizia, Lithuania, Turkmenistan, Armenia, Latvia and Estonia.

It is of interest to note that all 15 union republics have borders with other countries which will facilitate their secession from the union, should they desire it. Indeed, the close proximity of the Baltic republics of Lithuania, Latvia and Estonia to Finland and the Scandinavian countries may be one of the major motives encouraging the extremely strong drive of these republics to independence. There are of course other very important reasons, but the geographical position will certainly render their separation from the union much easier. Indeed, on 11 March 1990 the newly elected republican parliament of Lithuania, with more than a two thirds majority of nationalist members (belonging to the Sajudis party), voted by 124 votes to none (with six abstentions) to secede from the union. At the same parliamentary meeting a non-communist president of the republic was elected and the words 'Soviet Socialist' were removed from the republic's name.

Although the right to secede is nominally guaranteed by the constitution, the votes for these and other changes were considered to be largely symbolic and the actual detachment of the republic from the Soviet Union still depends on the goodwill of the Soviet Union's leaders and very difficult political and economic negotiations. Indeed, Moscow showed its hand very quickly by declaring that Lithuania will have to pay some several billion roubles to cover past investment in Lithuanian industry and non supply of ordered goods as part of the price for its independence. To this was added a threat to cut off oil supplies and to charge for raw materials at world market prices rather than the knocked down prices that Soviet industry today enjoys under the command economy. These verbal battles eventually reached a higher pitch, but that is another question beyond the purview of this book.

The Supreme Soviet (the word 'Soviet' means simply 'Council') of the Republic of Georgia also took drastic measures on 21 March 1990 when, in a 15 minute session, it voted to postpone republican elections for several months in order to allow for the registration of various political parties which would then be able to fight the elections. This was decided immediately after the Georgian parliament abolished the leading role of the communist party within the republic, in line with the earlier decision of the Congress of People's Deputies.

In addition to the union republics there are further political-administrative divisions into what are known as Autonomous Soviet Socialist Republics (ASSR), Autonomous *Oblasts* (regions) and Autonomous *Okrugs* (districts). The ASSRs are partially self governing republics based on the minority nationality of their population. The same nationality aspect serves as the raison d'être for the *oblasts* and *okrugs*, although their own powers are even fewer than the limited ones allowed to the ASSRs. An example of an autonomous *oblast* that comes to mind because of its recent prominence in the media is Nagorno-Karabach, the Armenian (Christian) enclave situated in the mainly Moslem SSR of Azerbaidzhan. These ASSRs, regions and districts are federated within the union republic in which they are situated. The RSFSR, for example, includes within the area of its federation 16 of the 20 ASSRs, five of the eight *oblasts* and all ten *okrugs*. The Chamber of Nationalities (see the section on 'Parliament' below) is constituted by representatives of the union republics (32 deputies each), the ASSRs (11 deputies each), the *oblasts* (five deputies each) and one deputy from each of the ten *okrugs*. In this way, it is believed, each nationality is fairly represented.

The political (constitutional) system

Freedom of speech

Opponents of written constitutions are able to find much succour in the constitution of the USSR which has, in the past, convincingly proved its inability to protect the rights of Soviet citizens. That change has occurred in the last few years is due not so much to the amendments that have been introduced as to the will of the country's leaders to pay more than lip service to the tenor of the written word. Although the basic changes that have been seen in the commercial laws are related to *Perestroika*, the most evident indication of the new system is attributable to its partner, *Glasnost* (openness). Freedom of speech and expression have become a permanent fixture of the Soviet scene.

People are no longer afraid to express their own opinions openly. The threat of being carted off to a *Gulag* or to a psychiatric institution on some specious pretext has virtually disappeared and political prisoners are now almost non-existent. The release of the late Andrei Sakharov, the great standard bearer of freedom, from internal exile in the town of Gorky was the signal to the people that they could raise their voices in protest. Indeed, anyone watching one of the channels of Soviet state television towards the end of January 1990 would have been able to see a long programme dedicated to the memory of Sakharov, a good part of which consisted of excerpts from an American television film, made several years ago (while Sakharov was still in Gorky), that graphically described the events leading up to the ignominious arrest and exile of the brave scientist who refused to be cowed by the threats of the KGB. The insidious behaviour of that organisation's officers at that time was there for all to see and this would have been unimaginable even two years earlier.

Another aspect of the new openness is the daily evening broadcasting of parliamentary debates. The parliament itself retains the right to decide that certain items will not be shown to the public. Indeed at the time of the debate, on 14 and 15 March 1990, on the constitutional amendments relating to the new post of executive president (see below) an argument arose during which the prime minister was accused of being involved in a scandal surrounding the affairs of a certain state cooperative organisation: the prime minister threatened to resign and it was moved that the debate should not be televised. The motion was defeated by a large majority and the Soviet public was given the chance to see parliamentary work in action.

Parliament

The familiar sight of a vast hall full of dark suited (mainly) men all raising their hands together with military precision in response to a call to vote on this or that matter is now an historical phenomenon. The day of the dissenter has, after a long wait, arrived in the assemblies of the state parliament and union parliaments throughout the Soviet Union.

The turning point came in December 1988 when the first serious constitutional change was introduced with a view to democratising the parliamentary system. The new style Congress of People's Deputies has 2,250 members, of which one-third represent constituencies. For this purpose the whole country is divided into voting areas which cut across ethnic and republican borders. They each have a population of roughly 300,000, one-third represent nationalities and the remaining third represent social organisations. Each deputy is elected for five years.

Deputies representing the nationalities are elected by the populace of the various federal units, the number of deputies returned by each unit depending basically on its size, varying from one to 32 (see 'Geography and Demography' above). The elections of representatives of the constituencies and nationalities may be contended by any candidate without reference to any particular organisation (although the vast majority of candidates in the first elections were either members of the communist party or otherwise sanctioned by it) but this is not true of the remaining 750 deputies which comprise elected representatives of specified all-union organisations ie, the communist party, trade unions, collective farms and consumer cooperatives (each of which is represented by 100 deputies) and six other groups which each return 75 deputies. These are: *Komsomol* (the All-Union Leninist League of Communist Youth), labour and military veterans, scientific, women's, cultural and a group on behalf of other miscellaneous organisations. The composition of this group of deputies somewhat dilutes the democratic basis of the parliament as a whole. However, in consequence of a constitutional amendment passed in December 1989, certain changes will be introduced in the next elections that should reduce still further the influence of these groups.

Although according to the constitution (as amended in 1988) the Congress of People's Deputies is the highest state organ of power (a two thirds majority vote of this congress is required to introduce amendments to the Soviet constitution), the retention in the constitution of the now famous Article 6 ensured that the various organs of the communist party of the Soviet Union remained. This situation has now been drastically altered as we shall discuss below.

The Congress of People's Deputies is due to meet at least once annually (although it may be convened extraordinarily as it was for four days in March 1990 to debate the constitutional amendments required to create an executive presidency and end the special role of the communist party), and is charged with the election, from amongst its own members, of a 450 strong Supreme Soviet the members of which sit on a full time basis. In fact, after the first national elections under the new system that were held in the spring of 1989, the procedure for electing the

450 had not been finalised and a preprepared list was proposed and approved. (Old habits die hard – although it should be mentioned that Andrei Sakharov was among the 450.) One fifth of the Supreme Soviet is to be elected annually on a rotation basis.

This new Supreme Soviet is a different animal from the one that existed prior to the 1988 constitutional amendments. The earlier version was little more than a rubber stamp for the approval of measures that were introduced by the Central Committee of the communist party. The new version is a proper parliament, special committees and commissions of which meet daily. The open and often rowdy debates of the Supreme Soviet sessions (which now take place every spring and autumn, for two or three months at a time, not for two or three days as in the case of its predecessor) are televised every evening for all to see. It must be hoped that this particular public manifestation of democracy will not lead to disenchantment with the system! For the first time in its history, the Soviet Union has what can almost be described as a parliamentary democracy, even though it still falls short of the western conception of such a system.

During its extraordinary session in March 1990 the Congress of People's Deputies did pass, by the required two thirds majority, the constitutional amendment according to which the new position of executive president was created. This gave the person holding that post powers far in excess of those held by the former 'president' who was actually Chairman of the Supreme Soviet (then Mikhail Gorbachev). The post of executive president is more on a par with that of the president of the United States or France. The debate on the bill created a coalition of old hard liners and progressive politicians both of which groups fear, for different reasons, the concentration of too much power in one pair of hands. The proposal was formulated by President Gorbachev who also holds the post of General Secretary of the communist party. His political instincts seem to have told him that with the amendment of Article 6 of the constitution (which is discussed below), the consequence of which is the abolition of the central role of the communist party, his other position, as president, must be converted into one where he will be given strong executive powers. This will enable him, or whoever else holds the post of president, to wield considerable influence over the policy making organs of the state.

The first executive president was elected by the Congress itself, for a period of five years. All subsequent elections will be direct ie, the populace itself will decide who the president will be. Only a 50 per cent plus one majority of Congress was required to elect the executive president and Mr Gorbachev was elected with a majority of 59.1 per cent of the members of the Congress.

The executive

The daily management of the Soviet Union rests in the hands of the Council of Ministers of the USSR, a rather cumbersome cabinet headed by a chairperson, known as the prime minister, who has eight deputies. The present incumbent is Mr Nikolai Ryzhkov. In the same way as the union republics have their own supreme soviet they also each have a council of ministers.

Ministers (including the prime minister), whether of the USSR or of the union republics are elected by their respective supreme soviets. Although in the past this has generally been prearranged, only two ministers of the USSR were elected unanimously in 1989, one of whom was Eduard Shevardnadze, the foreign minister. More remarkable is the fact that two ministers have lost their positions after a vote of no confidence. One of those ousted held the post of Minister of Culture and another was a deputy chairperson of the Council of Ministers who held the chair of the State Foreign Economic Commission. This commission advises the Ministry of Foreign Economic Relations on how it should conduct its affairs and its chair lost his position because of his objections to the reforms of the economic system.

The USSR Council of Ministers comprises about 100 members who are the USSR ministers, chairpersons of the union-republic councils of ministers and heads of state committees. The councils of ministers of the various union republics are similarly constituted. Each has a presidium which comprises the chair-person, deputy chairpersons and state committee heads and sets the agenda for meetings of the full council.

There are about 50 ministries and 20 state committees. The basic difference between ministries and state committees is that the former will deal with a specific field eg, finance, foreign affairs, defence, education, automobile industry, machine building, oil industry and transport, while a state committee will be responsible for across-the-board matters affecting all ministries such as supplies, planning, pricing, computer technology and, in the case of a newly-formed committee, questions affecting the nationalities. As in the case of ministries, there are state and union republic committees. The union republic committees, which are represented on the USSR Council of Ministers, are the apogee of an administrative pyramid whose base is at enterprise level and works upwards through local soviets.

The communist party

As has already been stated, the communist party of the Soviet Union derived its power from Article 6 of the Soviet constitution, which provided that:

> The leading and guiding force of Soviet society and the nucleus of its political system, of all state and public organisations, is the Communist Party of the Soviet Union (CPSU). The CPSU shall exist for the people and shall serve the people. The CPSU, on the basis of Marxism-Leninism, shall determine the general perspectives of the development of society and the direction of internal and foreign policy of the Soviet Union, shall direct the great constructive work of the Soviet people and shall provide a planned, systematic and theoretically well founded character for their *struggle for the victory of communism* (authors' emphasis) . . .

The words emphasised above have been singled out so as to demonstrate their blatantly anomalous place in the present movement of things in the Soviet Union. Even though Article 6 (together with several other articles) was, amended during the momentous March 1990 meeting of the Congress of People's Deputies just after it resolved to create the executive presidency,

thus drastically reducing the party's influence, it is still of importance to have knowledge of the situation as it was, if only better to
appreciate the very acute changes that have been introduced to
the Soviet system. It can do no harm to western business negotiators
to show their Soviet counterpart that they have some knowledge
of the local political system, particularly in the case in question.

It was originally believed that Article 6 would not be amended
until such a step was first approved by the party congress, which
was due to meet in the summer of 1990 (the central committee
already having approved the measure in February 1990). Such,
however, is the momentum of events in the Soviet Union that it
was decided to press forward without even letting the party's
rank and file having a real say in the matter. Now that Article 6,
in its old form has gone, there should be a drastic dilution of the
party's stranglehold on all branches of power. Once this has been
realised there should be something approaching a real separation
of powers ie, the effective separation of the legislative branch
(the Supreme Soviet and Congress of People's Deputies) from
the executive branch (the Council of Ministers) although the fact
that the new style executive president is chairman of the legislative assembly somewhat negates the validity of such a statement.

The constitutional amendments mean that equality has been
established between political parties, other social organisations
and popular fronts created within the framework of the constitution. Citizens are permitted to unite in political parties etc. and
the constitution 'guarantees' these bodies conditions in which
their aims may be successfully fulfilled. It remains to be seen how
these words will be transformed into practical changes.

Whether the separation of powers will work in the Soviet context still remains to be seen. The approximately 18 million members of the communist party, constituting about 7 per cent of the
population of the Soviet Union, may not give up their rights and
power without a struggle. It must be remembered that nearly all
the high political, military and bureaucratic posts are, and for
some time are likely to continue to be, held by party members.
There is no doubt, however, that feelings run high against the
party apparatus, as has been amply demonstrated by the recent
results in the local elections. It will be interesting to see to what

extent the party will be able or willing to maintain its sway over developments.

The hierarchy of the CPSU is pyramid-like, resting on a wide base of what are known as 'primary party organisations' to be found mainly in places of work throughout the Soviet Union. From here the organisation tapers upwards, rising through local area, regional and republic groups and committees and thence to the party congress, the Central Committee, the Secretariat of the Central Committee and culminating in the Politburo and the General Secretary, Mr Gorbachev.

The party congress meets about once every five years, the next, possibly fateful, meeting being set for summer 1990. Between congresses the Central Committee is the main discussion forum of the party. Discussion is indeed more active today than it has been at certain times in the past, particularly during Stalin's reign. Amongst its other functions the Central Committee elects (formally, at least) the Politburo and the General Secretary. The fact that the General Secretary sits both in the Central Committee and in the Politburo and heads the Secretariat which fixes the agenda for Politburo meetings will serve to emphasise the power that has been vested in one man. However, in view of the changes in the constitution, all this power may be rendered worthless. Hence the move to strengthen the authority of the president.

Perhaps the most important function of the Central Committee Secretariat is the appointment of both state and party officials under the system disparagingly known as *nomenklatura*. Nowhere, possibly, is the adage, 'It's not what you know but who you know' more appropriate. This deep-rooted system, where advance and promotion have been more likely to have been achieved because of one's connections rather than one's ability, is probably the major cause of the widespread inefficiency and corruption that are so much the bane of the Soviet Union. Of course, one of the best ways to achieve prominence has been to become a party member and work one's way up through the machinery, but the abrogation of Article 6 is likely to cause a serious blow to future advancement by this method. In fact, under the ever changing circumstances, a growing number of people are resigning their membership of the party. Whether this is simply because of dis-affection with party politics or as a means of protection against future recriminations that may be aimed at party members under some future administration, is difficult to say. Whatever the reason, however, the resignations do not bode well for the party's future.

Dissidence within the party has come to the surface with the advent of *glasnost*. There can be few in the west today who have not heard of Mr Boris Yeltsin, the former head of the party in Moscow who was dismissed from that post by the conservatives for his active criticism of their opposition to reforms. However, Mr Yeltsin found his way back to an influential position by using the new system in two different manners: first he was elected to the Congress of People's Deputies and then to the Supreme Soviet; subsequently, he was also elected to the Congress of People's Deputies of the Russian Federation, where he has since been elected as president of the republic.

To this must be added mention of another important dissident group within the party, the Democratic Platform which could very well form the nucleus of a future political party within a multi-party system that many people now see as inevitable.

Local politics

The soviet is the basic organ of government throughout the USSR, commencing with the USSR Supreme Soviet and the 15 supreme soviets of the union republics and filtering down through the soviets of the *oblasts*, *okrugs*, cities, towns and villages.

The extent of the power of these soviets has been very limited. Because of the communist doctrine there was no opportunity for the local soviets to run their own independent budgets, until the introduction of the very latest legislation on local self-depen-dence. Their only source of income until now has been a sales tax but even this, because of the extremely centralised system, has found its way into the country's central kitty. Whether the recent innovations, which will include property taxes being paid into the local, rather than central, kitty are going to cause a change remains to be seen, although it should be said that there has already been a limited amount of devolution of power from the centre. In any event, the new property laws will lead to an increase in the number of property owners with a concomitant rise in the amount of property taxes to be collected.

Under the 1988 reforms, deputies are elected to local soviets for five years and may be elected for two consecutive terms.

Economic system

Why is the economy of a country as richly endowed as the Soviet Union is with natural resources and people in such a bad state? To answer this question (which is the one that faced Gorbachev when he took over the reins of power in 1985) we must have a brief look at Soviet economic history.

To claim that nothing has been achieved since 1917 would be tantamount to saying that the lot of the population today is no better than it was under the czars. Such a statement would simply be untrue. It cannot be denied that the communists succeeded (albeit with the use of some extremely undesirable methods) in dragging an underdeveloped country into the twentieth century and provided the Soviet people with education, housing and culture. But there can be no doubt today that the Marxist-Leninist concepts which formed the basis of the country's development and transformation into a modern industrial nation were suitable only up to a point and that despite the considerable advances that have been made, the free-market economies have left the command economies of the communist world far behind.

The original objectives of the country's leaders, most notably Stalin, were to organise a heavy industrial base that would eventually lead to an equalisation of the Soviet Union with the world's advanced industrial states. In a way, this has been achieved. Had it not been so, the USSR would not have been able to send the first man into space and would not have attained military equality (or even superiority in some fields) with the United States. The major vehicle for the advancement of Soviet industry was the famous five year plans, under which everything was sacrificed to the golden calf of industrial advancement. The problem was that the country was not able to adapt its methods to a changing world where heavy industry was gradually being replaced by more sophisticated systems which depended to an ever growing degree on high technology rather than manpower.

So why, if the system as originally devised was able to provide the means of advancement into the mid-twentieth century, has it not been able to adjust to the changes of the second half of the century or to provide its people with a good standard of living? Although in a work of this size and nature it is not possible to give a detailed answer to this question, it may be said that the Soviet Union has become the victim of its own highly centralised system. This created a Frankenstein bureacracy whose masters were unable to rid themselves of their doctrinaire shackles and desire to hold onto their jobs at any cost. The party bureaucracy became so entwined with the executive and with the management of business that it was difficult to distinguish the wood of economic objectives from the trees of nomenklatura and other party ills. The criterion for holding down a job was not management skill or productivity but the ability to serve the party well. There was no incentive for the average worker (who under the heavily restricted entry procedures and politics found it difficult to join the party and whose pay was subject to wage levelling) to increase productivity, because he knew that he would not receive higher payment in return for greater effort. At the same time, the party member who toed the party line could not or would not use any initiative to change the system that was controlled by party dictates emanating from the Politburo.

The villain of the piece, as it were, was, and still is, *Gosplan*, the State Planning Commission. It is *Gosplan* that prepares, as it has done since the late 1920s, the five year plans that have become the bugbear of the Soviet economy. There is nothing intrinsically wrong with long term plans, provided that they are properly conceived and administered. Every well run business will have a plan based on its forecast for the coming years, taking into account possible market trends, material and labour costs, likely competition and all the other human and economic factors that are likely to affect its performance. It will not, however, set fixed production targets for its various products for the next five years without reference to these other factors because such an unwise policy is likely to lead to chaos and bankruptcy, as we shall now see.

The basic deficiency in the system has been that the goods to be manufactured and the levels of production have been determined without reference to demand. The various ministries prepare their lists of demands for the future stating eg, how many tractors, trucks, bicycles, pairs of shoes and water holding vessels are going to be ordered by them. *Gosplan* will then coordinate the demands of the several ministries and the required raw and other material allocations will be arranged by *Gossnab* (the State Committee for Material-Technical Supply).

It is this body that coordinates all stages of manufacture up to and including the finished product. In doing this it allocates the raw materials and other means in accordance with the directives approved by *Gosplan*, thereby closing off supply to other sources. This happens because each supplier will aim at producing the quantities it is obliged to supply to the preordained customers, although this does not always preclude over production of items that may not be required by the local market. Today, under the Law of State Enterprises, state enterprises are permitted to dispose of any production surplus to the best of their ability, whereas previously manufacturers had been obligated to return any surplus to the state kitty – although the state was not similarly obliged to take them.

We have chosen the expression 'water-holding vessel' above in order to illustrate a particular example of bad economics. The state will have decided how many of a certain item are to be produced, how many will be retailed, what the price will be and what wage will be paid. The product will then be produced by an uninterested producer while, at the same time, no-one has asked the consumers what they want ie, there has been no marketing. The only criteria facing the producer are how many and how much will it cost to produce them? The manufacturer will want to produce what is cost effective without reference to demand and he will be paid in any event. He has, for example, been ordered to produce a 'vessel holding three litres of water for household use'. He produces cost effective buckets but the consumer wants saucepans. Result: surplus of buckets and shortage of saucepans. This story will be repeated in relation to the whole gamut of products throughout the country and the mix up multiplied due to poor distribution: there will be stockpiles of unwanted goods in town A and shortages of the same goods in town B and vice versa. The end of the economic chain is virtually completed when the goods come off the production line. It is not surprising to find, therefore, that there may be a surplus of trucks without engines!

As a result of this system, where supply has not been suited to demand there have been shortages of some goods required by the populace and surpluses of other goods. And because of the lack of incentive and competition the quality of the goods produced is shoddy.

The Law of State Enterprises

A real solution to these problems has not yet been found but an attempt of sorts has been made at opening up the economy by the introduction of four laws; the Laws on Individual Labour, State Enterprises and Joint Ventures, all passed in 1987, and the Law on Cooperation which was enacted in 1988. We will briefly discuss here the Law on State Enterprises while the other three are discussed in detail in later chapters. All these laws are, to a certain extent, like patches sewn on to a very threadbare piece of clothing and will not prevent holes appearing elsewhere. They do however form the embryo of a free market system and their effect is already being felt. This does not mean, however, that a major upheaval of the system is not required and President Gorbachev has indicated his intention to introduce really radical reforms.

The Law on State Enterprises was the flagship of *Perestroika*. Its main objective was to convert state run industrial bodies into autonomous self financing corporations to be judged on their ability to make a profit. However, a close examination of the law will reveal that it is basically a huge contradition in terms hastily conceived and drafted. As is normally the case in the Soviet Union the law only deals in general principles, leaving the detail to evolve through trial and error.

On the credit side the Law on State Enterprises provides for the following free market concepts: self-financing; financial accountability; self-management; profits or losses serving as the indicator of success or failure, competition to be encouraged in order to fulfil consumers' demands; research and development funds to be created from profits; managers to be elected on a competitive basis and to be subject to dismissal by higher organs; workers to be paid according to results and according to category; no waste of energy supplies (such waste being a basic malady of the economy); bank financing to be made available; enterprises, as separate legal entities to have the right to enter directly into overseas trade activities without going through Soviet trade organisations (enterprises may also join together to form an association to represent them in foreign trade); penalties for causing pollution; introduction of a form of cost accounting and auditing; bankruptcy in the event of continued bad payment record or if the enterprise fails to find buyers for its goods.

That was the good news! On the debit side the following phenomena appear: activity of enterprises to be organised within the framework of the state plan as prepared by *Gosplan* and operated within the relevant branch of the state economy; the party organisation of the enterprise will be its political nucleus; the party organistion will bear responsibility with others for the selection, appointment and education of cadres at the enterprise – the enterprise is controlled by a ministry or some other government body which is also its highest organ; the economic guidelines for the enterprise are laid down by the Council of Ministers; the enterprise will produce in accordance with orders received from the state; continued central control of supply of raw materials; continued centralised fixing of prices; general subjection of enterprise to the five year plan.

This law was passed in 1987, only two years after Gorbachev took over the reins of power and bears all the hallmarks of an attempt to reform the system without rocking the boat. In practice, the attempt has not been very successful. It has proved impossible to impose elements of a free market on the rotting chassis of communism. Even though it is intended, in 1991, to dilute the effect of central planning by removing from the functions of *Gosplan* and *Gossnab* the micro economic elements and have them concentrate instead only on macro activities, and to overhaul the pricing and taxation systems, it is clear to anyone who has seen a queue for some product or another in the Soviet Union that a major revision of the whole basic system is required. In the meantime, however, the State Enterprise Law will, with all its warts, continue in force until the introduction of further anticipated major changes to accommodate the full development of a free market economy.

Foreign trade and free zones

Other reforms have been introduced in the realm of foreign trade and in relation to free zones. The state monopoly on conducting foreign trade has been abolished and today this field of activity is open to all forms of associations, including cooperatives and joint ventures. The first step in the reorganisation of foreign trade was the formation of the State Commission for Foreign Economic Relations which oversees the operations of the new Ministry of Foreign Economic Relations (which was itself formed as a result of the merger of two other bodies, the Ministry of Foreign Trade and the State Foreign Economic Committee). The work of the Commission resulted in the passing of Decree 1405 of the USSR Council of Ministers in December 1988 which is discussed in detail in the chapter on joint ventures.

Another channel chosen for the purpose of trying to project the USSR into the new technological age and to open up the country's market is the Free Zone. The benefits usually accorded in zones such as these are available also in Soviet free zones together with some peculiarly Soviet benefits. These include exemptions from customs duties on imports to and exports from the zone, reduction of customs duties on goods produced in the free zone and imported to the internal market of the USSR, supply of labour force and introduction of simplified recruitment and dismissal procedures and application of free market prices within the zone. These benefits are available to all investors in the zone, local or foreign, and there are additional benefits available to foreign investors only including exemption from tax on repatriated profits, investment protection whereby rouble component of profits may be converted into foreign currency (at the market rate of the bank operating in the zone), simplified entry and residency procedures for foreigners, guarantees in the USSR market for goods manufactured in the zone and free selection of financial sources for operations in the zone, including overseas funds.

The use of the free zone in the USSR is to be more far reaching than is usual in other countries where the contact between the zone itself and the hinterland is more tenuous and generally geared only to the export market. The objectives of the zones in the USSR, however, are to assist in the whole restructuring of the Soviet economy by contributing to key areas such as supply of advanced technology, modern management skills, and better quality consumer goods. For this purpose two types of zone are envisaged ie, complex zones where there would be concentration of new production methods for the internal market and development of the respective economic planning region (the Russian Federation, for example, is divided into 10 economic planning regions ie, North-West, Central, Central Black Earth, Volgo-Vyatka, Volga, North Caucasus, Ural, West Siberia, East Siberia and the Far East,); 'functional' zones where the accent should be first on the development of new equipment and second on tourism and the storage of goods in transit ie, the usual type of free zone established other countries. The functioning of zones catering for the purposes of both of these types is also a possibility.

The first free zones to be established are in Nakhodka, which is in the far East economic region and is attracting attention fiom Japan, China, Singapore and South Korea, and in Vyborg in the Leningrad area which should facilitate Soviet-Scandinavian contacts. It is interesting to note that both these zones are within the area of the RSFSR and one wonders if this is purely coincidental or has been planned with ulterior motives in mind. Three further zones envisaged are Sakhalin Island in the far East, Chita Region in Siberia and Leningrad.

Currency

The rouble deserves a little attention. The basic problem of the currency is its inconvertibility. This is one of the major obstacles facing Mr Gorbachev and it is quite likely that a drastic move will be made to render it a convertible currency before the end of 1990. As to the rate of exchange, there are several, starting with the unrealistic official one according to which the rouble is on a par with the pound sterling. Towards the end of 1989, a new tourist rate was introduced which devalued the rouble, for tourists only, by 1000 per cent! A tourist will now receive 10 roubles for every pound he changes at the official exchange offices, although there is little or nothing that a tourist or businessperson may do with the roubles (see 'General Hints and Advice'). There is also the black market rate which is approximately twice the tourist rate.

The rouble is the currency of the whole Soviet Union although Estonia intends to introduce its own Krona in January 1991 as a first step to convertibility.

Ecological awareness

Before we leave the economic sphere there should be a mention of the ecological problems facing the Soviet Union. The name Chernobyl will be known to all readers. The fact that the disaster occurred and caused such extensive damage and confusion is indicative of the lack of attention that has been given to ecological matters in the USSR (not that the rest of the world has a great deal to be proud of). Two other, less well-known ecological black marks are the virtual destruction of the Aral Sea in central Asian USSR and the pollution of Lake Baikal in SE Siberia, the largest freshwater lake in Eurasia and also the world's deepest. The lake has suffered what is believed to be irreversible damage as a result of the activities of chemical industries around its shores.

Although there is an awakening of a green conscience, it is still much overshadowed by far greater economic problems. It is unlikely that these problems will find a real solution until the old system is completely dissolved and replaced by a true free market economy. Even then it will prove difficult to close down environmentally dangerous industries if this is likely to cause unemployment. In the meantime the old system has collapsed and a void exists which is only slowly being filled. Unless this situation is rapidly rectified the country will become fraught with danger, and it is more than likely that the newly elected executive president's first priority will be to use his increased power to introduce far more radical changes to the economy than would have seemed possible only months ago.

Banking system

The banking system in the USSR is very backward by western standards, despite reforms carried out in 1988. The central bank *(Gosbank)* which coordinates the operations of the other state banks is the pivot of the system. The other banks, which deal in specific fields are: *Vnesheconombank* or the Bank for Foreign Economic Relations, which deals, as its name implies, in matters relating to foreign trade; *Zhilsotsbank* or the Bank for Housing, Municipal Services and Social Development, which provides credit for projects such as residential developments, cultural and educational establishments and even for associations such as dog-lovers' clubs, is the main banker to the cooperative movement; *Promstroibank* which is the Industrial and Capital Investment Bank, finances industrial construction and capital equipment acquisition; *Sberbank* or the Bank for Savings and Credits for the People, which is exactly what its name suggests, a personal savings bank for individuals which also extends credit to its customers within the limited confines allowed by Soviet law; *Agroprombank* which is the Agro-Industrial Bank which serves mainly as the banker for organisations operating in that sector.

The foreign business person is most likely to come into contact with *Vnesheconombank* which even has a branch in Zurich and correspondents throughout the world. This is the bank that will provide foreign currency credits or guarantees to and for joint ventures. In its normal activities it deals in documentary credits and collections.

Under the 1988 reforms, a new form of commercial bank was introduced. Such a body may be set up by the equivalent of shareholders who are usually organisations operating in a particular sector which will then be served by the bank. Individuals cannot acquire the shares which, as a rule, have a nominal value of R 100,000 each. The banks will extend credits to the sector by which it was founded. Cooperatives are also permitted to set up banks and this aspect is discussed in more detail in chapter 3.

Legal system

The non-separation of powers has been no more evident in the Soviet Union than in the absence of an independent judiciary. It has not been uncommon, for example, for a judge to call a local official at the Communist party to obtain guidance before reaching a decision. Such a state of affairs is anathema to a free society and recognition of this fact is evident in the changes that have been introduced in the wake of the nineteenth party conference held in 1988, where Mikhail Gorbachev, a law graduate himself pushed for reform of the legal system.

New norms of procedure came into force on 1 December 1989 although the implementation of the revolutionary (by Soviet standards) provision in Article 7 was postponed until 1 July 1990. The article provides that:

> Citizens of the Soviet Union have the right to court protection from illegal acts of state controlled bodies and official persons and also from any infringement or any violation of their dignity or honour, life and health, to personal freedom and property, to other rights and liberties envisaged by the constitution of the USSR, constitutions of union republics, constitutions of autonomous republics and Soviet laws . . .

Two other important provisions are contained in Articles 8 and 11. The former declares the independence of the courts (in recognition of the principle of separation of powers) while the latter allows for the introduction of something approaching a jury system. Cases in Soviet courts are heard by a panel of three, one of whom is a professional judge while the other two are people's representatives, normally elected at places of work. Judges are elected, for limited periods of time, by soviets – the USSR

Supreme Soviet in the case of Supreme Court judges, the union republic supreme soviet in the case of union republic supreme courts and local soviets where lower courts are concerned. Under the proposed new system, which has yet to be implemented, there will be an extended number of people's representatives who will serve as a jury of sorts but only in cases involving a minimum penalty exceeding ten years' imprisonment.

In civil matters, particularly those involving complicated commerical aspects a dispute would normally come before a panel of the State Arbitration Service. If a foreigner is concerned the case would normally be heard, in accordance with the parties' prior agreement, by an overseas arbitrator, usually in Stockholm.

Time alone will tell if the reforms referred to will achieve their objectives but with the introduction of the economic and political changes it must be hoped that the legal system will also enter the realm of freedom and justice and adapt to the new situation.

Bureaucracy

The *chinovnik*, the government official, became the most characteristic figure in Russian life. The bureaucratic machine seemed to have discovered the secret of perpetual motion: spewing forth an ever mounting volume of papers, multiplying in size at a geometrical rate, feverishly producing new departments and sub departments for yet more hosts of underpaid and corrupt officials . . . bribery, embezzlement, speculation of every kind were now part of everyday life of the elephantine mechanism. (Tibor Szamuely, 'The Russian Tradition', London, 1974)

This description of the Russian bureaucracy as it developed under Czar Nicholas I could serve just as well to draw a picture of the sorry state of affairs today in the Soviet Union. Of all the ills of communism, the bureaucracy may prove to be the least curable. The fact that it is endemic in the country may prevent its successful removal. It cannot be legislated against as in the case of political, economic or legal problems and its future is really dependent on the manner in which the other basic changes affect daily life. It

would be no an exaggeration to say that the acid test of success or
failure of the reforms that have already been introduced and
those that will surely come in the near future is the extent to
which they manage to overcome the obstacles that will almost
certainly be placed in their way by the bureaucratic army which
will not relinquish its position without a fight.

Perhaps it would be truer to say that the government itself will
find it difficult to disband or drastically reduce this army because
of the serious unemployment problem that would arise. Perhaps
Gorbachev will fail where others have failed.

The size of this book and the time available have not enabled
us to prepare a detailed study of the bureaucracy. We have
decided, instead, to provide the reader with a glimpse of the type
of bureaucratic journey required to be taken by the Soviet partner
in a joint venture in order to file an application for approval of the
venture, in this case, by the Moscow City Council. (The foreign
partner should dismiss all brave intentions of trying to beat the
bureaucracy.) The full details relating to the formation of joint
ventures are discussed later and here we are merely emphasising
the micro bureaucratic procedure.

The decision of at least eight different offices will be required
to be seen by the city council. For this purpose, of course, all the
foundation documents of the joint venture will have to be delivered to and reviewed by these offices. The names of the offices
are as follows:

1 Main Directorate of Science and Technology, in respect of
   technical and technological solutions.
2 Main Directorate of Architecture, in respect of providing land
   for construction, reconstruction, and structural maintenance of
   buildings.
3 Main Registry of Floor Space, in respect of providing (office
   and residential) space for joint venture and its employees.
4 Moscow Town Planning Authority, in respect of payments by
   the joint venture into the currency fund of Moscow City Council
   and provision of employment by the joint venture for workers
   in connection with capital investment and construction.
5 Moscow City Council of Gosnab, in respect of material-technical
   supplies to the joint venture.

6 Foreign Trade Company MOSINTER, in respect of supplying forms of cooperation, drawing up of statutory documents and checking calculations of economic effectiveness.
7 Moscow Environment Committee, in respect of ecological protection of city.
8 Main Financial Directorate of Moscow, in respect of financial stability of Soviet partner.

The above names are translated from a form on which each of the above offices will indicate its approval or rejection of the joint ventures credentials within its field of authority. One would hope that as the Soviet Union modernises it will find a way of, first, allowing entrepreneurs to start up a business with more ease and, secondly (in this particular case), of concentrating all matters touching on the validity of a joint venture with a foreign partner under one roof.

We will leave the bureaucracy here but will return to it in a more light-hearted frame of mind in our discussion of some of its facets that the unwary visitor to the Soviet Union may encounter. At this point we will turn to more specific business activities in the Soviet Union.

2

Setting up a cooperative

Introduction

Now we are to take another big step in the path of *Perestroika*: to give a broad base for the greatest assistance to the cooperative movement with its really enormous possibilities . . . The main feature of cooperation is that it is the most important social manifestation of independent action and the creative activity of people and their involvement into the direct management of economic and social processes on a regular democratic basis.

Thus spoke Nikolai Ryzhkov, Chairman of the USSR Council of Ministers (the prime minister) in the course of a report delivered on 24 May 1988 at a joint meeting of the Chamber of Unions and Chamber of Nationalities during the ninth session at the old USSR Supreme Soviet.

The significance of the above words is, perhaps, lost in their verbosity. What Mr Ryzhkov was saying was that the Soviet Union had enacted a law which created a legal entity similar, in some respects, to a private company, with democratic organs, which, it was hoped, would serve as a springboard to private entrepreneurial business activities.

The Law on Cooperation, as in the Law on Joint Ventures which will be discussed later in the book, adopts language which one would not find in say, English laws, except perhaps in a government White Paper explaining the object of the law.

Article 10 of the Law starts with the words: 'Membership of cooperatives is voluntary'. This is to emphasise the freedom of choice, which is so new to Soviet citizens that it has to be spoon fed to them. The same article explains that state or other bodies are not permitted to interfere in the economic or other activities of cooperatives. Then comes an admonishment to anyone who might wish to try his luck in a cooperative venture, that cooperatives are liable for their losses ie, you cannot rely on the State to salvage you from a financial mess. Just in case this does not convince, Article 8 also categorically states that the state is not responsible for the cooperative's debts. This article, after describing a number of specific activities that cooperatives may engage in culminates with another exhortation, this time to 'Soviets of People's Deputies and other State bodies', to assist cooperatives in developing joint enterprises and organisations. (The article heading refers to 'Principles' of activity and not to 'Type' of activity as does Article 3 referred to below)

The word cooperative is, to western eyes, misleading. The use of this term was, however, more preferable in the Soviet Union than, say, private company, in facilitating adoption of the Law on 1 July 1988. This date may be considered as one of *Perestroika's* important milestones.

In a more direct passage the Chairman of the Council of Ministers stated that the main line of development of cooperation lies through the exchange of products and money 'on a business-like commercial basis in an environment of economic competitiveness'. This was, indeed, a revolutionary thing to say but it is impossible to ignore some of the more serious obstacles that the 'revolution' has faced.

First, imagine fledglings in the nest that for several weeks have been fed by their parents without having to fend for themselves. Through some misfortune the parents have been lost to their progeny before these have developed into fully fledged birds able to leave the nest. For 70 years the Soviet economy had been fed from above by a series of five-year plans, economic directives and other centralised orders. No one had had to think or fend for himself or herself. Suddenly, the people are being told, 'Go forth – here is your big chance to escape the fetters of centralisation' – all without either real experience or tradition or any established mechanism.

Secondly, the new 'entrepreneur', having decided to take the plunge before his wing feathers are fully developed, free falls to a barren land full of rocks and boulders in the form of the bureaucratic machine which, as we have seen, has not yet been dismantled. Permits are still required for this or that activity, and the permit givers are people who are used to the mechanised execution of orders reaching them from the centre and which are then directed by them to the periphery. The word 'creativity' is absent from their vocabulary and they find it very difficult to deal with either the decentralisation of the apparatus or the independent air of cooperatives.

Finally, the change of the whole economic mechanism of the country to conditions of self financing is slower than is desirable. The fledgling that had been used to receiving its food in the form of subsidies is now unable to rely on that source. The old system is breaking down faster than the new one is developing and, in order not to leave a vacuum, the old system is being kept in place during 1990 with big, important changes expected in 1991. As a matter of interest there are still some 800 bureaucratic rules and regulations which conflict, in one way or another, with the Law on Cooperation.

All these obstacles (to which should be added objective material difficulties such as. a shortage of buildings and vital equipment) are, hopefully, of a transient nature and should, in time, be overcome either by custom or by legislation. There is little doubt now that there is a strong drive toward independent activity as may be seen from the facts and figures on cooperatives. At the end of 1989, 5.5 million people were engaged directly by over 210,500 cooperatives and there has been remarkable growth rate since the introduction of the Law. (If the direct relatives of these people are taken into account nearly twenty million people (about 7 per cent of the population) are already affected, directly or indirectly, by the cooperative movement and the growth rate is remarkable. In 1989 alone the number of active cooperatives increased nearly threefold while the number of employees was four times greater at the end of 1989 than twelve months earlier. Sales during this period increased over sixfold to 40 billion roubles in 1989. All this tends to lead to the conclusion that the 1988 legis-lation has at least provided a sound basis and framework for the formation of legal entities from which direct state interference is absent.

It is worthy of note that the production cooperative movement is now represented in parliament by its chairman, Vladimir Tikhonov, who was elected in the 1989 elections.

Cooperatives had existed in the Soviet Union prior to the enactment of the 1988 Law on Cooperation. They were established on an individual basis ie, each cooperative devised its own individual statutes which required special approval. They dealt mainly in manufacturing, restaurants, cafes and scrap. A forerunner to the Law on Cooperation was the Law on Individual Labour Activity passed in 1986. This law enabled individual Soviet citizens to work privately and established businesses on a purely independent basis. One of its major objectives was to enable people such as students, housewives and pensioners to find legal work ie, to legalise moonlighting. Some of the activities that have attracted private initiative are taxi driving, painting and decorating, language teaching and other private tuition, and dressmaking. Each person wishing to operate under the law has to obtain a permit from the local municipal body and the price of a permit is based on potential future earnings. For example a taxi-driver will be asked for about R 600 annually.

Types of permitted activity

It is important to understand that the major objective of the new political-economical-legal laws is to improve means of production and to open the Soviet economy to all forms of economic competition. The Law of Cooperation, therefore, provides (Article 3) that cooperatives may participate in any kind of activity except those expressly proscribed by the law of the USSR or any of the Union Republics. Although this provision is so basic in free countries it is a revolutionary concept in Soviet terms, where the general norm is that citizens are prohibited from doing anything unless it is expressly permitted by law.

What, therefore, is a cooperative permitted to engage in? The Law on Cooperation sets out a quite comprehensive list of activities that are divided broadly into producing and consumer fields. The specific activities are: the manufacture of products and goods; provision of services to third parties (whether state or private); production and processing of agriculture products, machinery and equipment and consumer goods; recycling unwanted waste materials and scrap; repair and maintenance of equipment; services for manufacturing industries road and residential construction, retail trade, restaurants and food outlets; other services including medical assistance, legal services, transport (trucks); scientific research, design, sport, fishing, and allied activities, mining, forestry, timber processing and other spheres of economic activity.

However, 'What the Lord giveth the Lord taketh away'. The following activities are presently out of bounds for cooperatives:

- manufacturing, buying and selling of gold and precious metals and precious stones or goods where such materials may be used e.g. teeth;

- gambling establishments, lotteries and saunas;

- manufacture of weapons and ammunition and weapon repair;

- manufacture of alcoholic beverages;

- organisation of educational institutions;

- manufacture and sale of food containing additives the use of which is prohibited by state medical authorities;

- maintenance and service of state broadcasting services;

- manufacture of medals and state decorations, seals and stamps;

- hard currency transactions;

- pawnbroking;

- manufacture, repair or sale of icons and religious artefacts;

- manufacture and sale of non-decorative candles;

- provision of certain medical services, eg, dentists using gold; all surgery including abortion, cases involving cancer, infectious diseases, venereal diseases and skin ailments, drug addiction, or mental illness; emergency cases; birth control and pregnancy;

- pharmaceutical manfacture and sale;

- reproduction of films and videos or dealing in connection therewith.

Certain other activities are permitted only upon reaching agreement with the particular state body for which such activity is the main one. These include editorial and publishing services, printing of forms, medical assistance, organisation of public spectacles such as pop concerts, manufacture of duplicating equipment, recording on gramophone records or tapes and other fields such as tourism and the leisure activities.

The prohibitions or restrictions are aimed either at preserving state monopolies or at maintaining strict controls or production levels. The sale of non-decorative candles, for example, may seem an odd exception. However, if one considers that these cost about one kopek to manufacture and sell for about R 3-5 it becomes more comprehensible that the government wishes to hold on to this particular business. Other items are included because of the state's difficulty in shaking off its security paranoia eg, manufacture of rubber stamps and of duplicating equipment. In future though, it is expected that these lists will become considerably shorter. The prohibitions did not actually appear in the Law on Cooperation as enacted but were originally read into it from the Law on Individual Labour Activity (articles 13, 16 and 19). They were however institutionalised as part of the Law on Cooperation by a decree of the Council of Ministers of 29 December 1988.

Notwithstanding these restrictions the cooperatives, as we will see, serve as an important vehicle in the transformation from centralisation to free market orientation.

Property ownership

Cooperatives are allowed to acquire property for their own purposes. This may sound rather trite but it is revolutionary in Soviet terms. By Article 7 of the Law on Cooperation, a cooperative is granted the right to own property including buildings, machinery, equipment, means of transportation, goods, financial means and other property as may be required to achieve the goals of its activity.

It would appear that, if Article 7 is read in conjunction with Decree 412 of the Council of Ministers of 18 May 1989, a cooperative may also own property abroad including, for example, shares in a foreign company. Decree 412 which relates to 'The Development of Overseas Activities of Soviet Organisations' provides, among other things, that Soviet state enterprises and private cooperatives are entitled to enter into joint ventures abroad and for that purpose to invest foreign currency. Upon obtaining the required permit and registering with the relevant authority a cooperative would, therefore, be able to invest in a foreign business. Once a permit is granted the requisite hard currency would be made available.

Creation of cooperatives

The creation of a cooperative is effective upon registration of its statutes. No permission is required from any official body. These apparently innocent words which constitute the basis of the provisions of Article 11 of the Law on Cooperation are remarkable in a country where one's every act has been conditional on receiving the permit of a state, economic or other body. Any three or more people aged 16 or over, the 'founders' (or 'promoters' to use the expression found in the English Companies Act) may join together to form a cooperative. They merely have to fulfil the provisions of the Law on Cooperation and they will have their legal entity through which they are able to do business and, hopefully, profit.

Under Article 11, the application to register the statutes is filed with the executive committee of a borough, city or regional council of deputies, depending on the intended location of the cooperative's head office. The executive committee of the respective council of deputies will then consider the statutes within one month of filing to determine whether they comply with the law. Registration may be refused only in the event of non compliance ie, there is no discretionary power. Failure to register within the one-month period entitles the applicants to file an administrative complaint to the executive committee of a higher council of deputies, who must examine the complaint within 15 days. Outright refusal to register the statutes may be appealed against either to one of the higher executive committees or to the courts. The appeal must be considered within one month.

The cooperative system is open to all individuals (subject to the restriction that no individual may be the chairman of two or more cooperatives of the same type), a state organisation or another cooperative (which may set up a subsidiary). In the case of individuals it is conceivable that a family would set up a co-operative which would be equivalent to a family company or partnership in England. If a state or cooperative organisation wishes to establish a cooperative it must obtain the written consent of its manager, for example, where an industrial state enterprise wishes to exploit a technological advance in a more productive manner. The cooperative would obtain the rights to apply the technology in production and then use its own financial resources, technical support, working space and order books to exploit this technology in a purely business-like manner. In acting in this way it would be able to free itself from the strictures of central control and possibly avoid years of delay. Article 26 of the Law on Cooperation specifically encourages the establishment of scientific and technological groups to carry out research and development and to apply the research in production and proposes tax benefits for such operations.

Just as a reminder that Big Brother is still in the background, a cooperative that will have to use land or other natural resources in connection with its production activities will have to obtain the written consent for their provision either from the relevant state authority or from the main tenant as a prerequisite to registration.

Statutes of a cooperative

Strangely, the Law on Cooperation gives no indication whatsoever as to the required contents of the statutes of a cooperative. By comparison, the English Companies Acts provide both general directives and sample documents. This vacuum has been filled by custom that developed in the pre-Law period where several cooperatives were approved on an ad hoc basis. These carried on business, among other things, as recyclers of secondary raw materials, food outlets and producers of consumer goods.

The form of statutes approved for these pre-Law cooperatives today serve as precedents for the statutes of new cooperatives. Their contents must reflect the following:

- name of the cooperative

- location of its head office;

- its objects and aims;

- rules for admission to and dismissal and resignation from membership;

- rights and obligations of members;

- management and control organs;

- rules for acquisition of property;

- rules for distribution of profits;

- rules for reorganisation and termination of activities.

Membership of cooperative

Membership is open to any person over the age of 16. The Law, by adopting the term 'any person', seems not to limit membership to Soviet citizens. This view is strengthened by the norms of the Law on the Legal Position of Foreign Citizens in the USSR of 1981 which provide that certain activities are permitted to be carried out by foreign citizens where they are not specified as being available to Soviet citizens alone.

A person may be employed by and/or become a member of a cooperative even though he may have another main place of work and, unless he is a manager of a factory, a member of the police force, a judge or holder of some other official post, he will not require any special permission from his place of work. This is a privileged exception to general labour legislation according to which, if someone wishes to work in secondary employment, a special notice is required to be given and references must be obtained from the primary employer. The aim of the new provision is to encourage as many people as possible to become involved in cooperatives.

There is also another class of members known as 'collective members'. A collective member may be eg, a state or collective organisation or another cooperative. We have already given the example of a state organisation which may set up a subsidiary cooperative to serve as the organ for exploiting new technology. This type of structure also tends to bring about a gradual shifting of the enterprise to a cooperative footing. A specific example of large state cooperatives is 'FORMULA 7', which was set up by a state organisation with the specific objective of exploiting scientific advances and applying them in industry.

Rights and obligations of members

The rights and obligations of members of cooperatives are governed by article 13 of the Law and they include a right to share in profits and to receive information on the cooperative's activities. The article imposes obligations to take part in the administration of the cooperative, to preserve its property and perform its commitments. There are other rights which are not specified and are linked to the member's employment by the cooperative. These include the right to vacation and to social security and will be discussed in more detail below. Further obligations may be imposed by the cooperatives.

Control and management

The supreme organ of the cooperative is the general meeting which will elect a chair who will be responsible for managing the regular business of the cooperative. In 'large' (undefined in the Law) cooperatives a board will also be elected by the general meeting to assist the chair.

The matters that come within the purview of the authority of the general meeting are:

- adoption of the statutes (or any amendments or additions to them);

- election of the chair, board and internal auditing commission;

- approval of members' entrance to and resignation and dismissal from the cooperative, and the size of a member's initial and subsequent ('share') contributions;

- adoption and amendment of rules of informal proceedings;

- regulation of the distribution of profits, application of funds and reserves and questions of price structure;

- regulation of pay and question of liability for damage caused to the cooperative's property;

- decisions on matters of reorganisation or termination of activity.

The Law is silent on the question of the size of the majority required in specific matters (contrast the Law on Joint Ventures which requires unanimous decisions in most matters) and therefore a simple majority is all that is needed to determine the above matters. Each member, including collective members, has only one vote without regard for the size of the contribution to the property of the cooperative. The chair (or, where there is a board, the board) oversees the day to day activities of the cooperative, represents it in contacts with outside parties and resolves questions which are not within the competence of the general meeting. This would include the registration and approval of agreements (normally two signatures would be required on behalf of the cooperative eg, those of the chairman and chief accountant).

Reorganisation and liquidation

Decisions on reorganisation (including merger and amalgamation) and (voluntary) liquidation of a cooperative are within the exclusive jurisdiction of the general meeting and therefore require a mere 51 per cent majority to be adopted. Theoretically this could mean that say, three members (of a four member co-operative) who have contributed 10 per cent to the property of the cooperative could (on the basis of one vote per member) defeat a fourth member who has contributed 90 per cent of the property.

The executive committee of the council of deputies that authorised the registration of the cooperative is also empowered to liquidate the cooperative if it is incurring losses or is insolvent or it has, despite a warning, repeatedly or grossly violated legis-lation eg, it has conducted prohibited business or concealed profits.

Appeal against a decision to liquidate the cooperative may be filed, within three months, to the next superior council of deputies or to the council of ministers of an autonomous republic or union republic, or with the court.

Unions of cooperatives

Cooperatives in various regions are entitled, under Article 16, to form unions (to avoid confusion with the use of the word 'union' elsewhere in this work, 'unions' will be referred to here as 'feder-ations') either within their own regions or union republics or statewide or as a federation of units carrying on the same type of business. For example, a federation of cooperatives was formed in Moscow in August 1987. Its object is to assist in better coordin-ation of activity, to study existing and future market trends as these may affect cooperatives, to protect its members' legal rights and to offer them legal assistance by representing their interests before appropriate state bodies and in international organisations. The Law recommends fields of activities for the federations, including the promotion of improvements in production and the drawing up of guidelines aimed at making the fullest use of avail-able reserves and potential in order to assist the growth of the cooperative movement. Such federations have promoted cooper-atives in international trade. Individual cooperatives contribute to the budgets of the federations.

Economic functioning of cooperatives

Article 17 of the Law sets out to emphasise the special position enjoyed by producing and consumer cooperatives by pointing out that:

- they are economically independent;
- they enjoy financial autonomy and are self-financing;
- they must decide production and sales levels for themselves;
- their relations with state and other bodies, organisations, and suppliers are all based solely on agreement which are free from state interference and which, in the event of dispute between the parties, may be sued upon by either party ie, regular free market contractual relationships exist between the parties.

The Law on Cooperation does not categorically state that the liability of its members is limited in any way and, theoretically, the courts would be able to determine that members are personally liable for the cooperative's obligations. At the time of publication, there is no known precedent imposing such liability, but the councils of deputies registering cooperatives now require information on the extent of the personal liability of each member, which would be determined by agreement between the founders.

Planning

Plans are ratified by the general meeting and, according to Article 18 of the Law, their basis is contracts with 'consumers of goods and suppliers of materials and technical resources'. It seems strange that a law would have to make such a comment but it is absolutely symptomatic of a fettered economy that has not managed to shake off its chains.

Further indication of this inability to make a break with the past or, perhaps more correctly, of the fact that the predominant factor is still the centralised system, is the second part of article 18. This directs that when a cooperative is preparing its plans it must take account of long-term state norms which include:

- price levels for goods manufactured (and services provided) and sold in carrying out state tenders;

- levels of tax payments;

- interest on bank loans;

- norms for payment for natural resources;

- fines for emission of pollutants into the environment;

- norms for deduction paid to national insurance fund;

Then come the words of relief: 'No other norms or basic planning indications are set out for the cooperatives'.

The use of the word 'norm' emphasises the continued influence of the state.

3

Operation of cooperatives

Pricing

The early months of cooperative activity revealed a problem which soon became the central issue in discussions on the social and economic effectiveness of cooperative organisations. A large segment of public opinion felt that cooperative prices were too high. On the other hand there was no doubt in people's minds that the quality of goods and services sold and provided by co-operatives was far superior to their state supplied alternatives. There were two major reasons for the higher prices. First there was and still is, a huge and indiscriminate demand for the goods on the domestic market (such is the hunger of the 'starved' Soviet consumer) and second, enterprising cooperatives were venturing into fields that were not adequately catered for by state enterprises.

This vexed question was dealt with quite adeptly in article 19 of the Law on Cooperation, which makes a clear distinction between two different situations ie, those where the state is somehow involved and those where the free market forces operate.

The general guideline is that prices should be a fair reflection of the underlying costs and that they should be fixed by independent agreement between the buyer (the consumer) and the seller (the cooperative). The object is to provide an incentive for the cooperative (by receiving a fair mark-up) and also to strive for improved production methods.

However, there are two situations where the state's involvement causes a digression from the 'independent agreement' aspect: where goods and services are provided under a state tender; where goods, manufactured from materials (raw or otherwise) supplied to the coperative from state sources (ie, at the wholesale prices set by *Gossnab* enterprises) are sold either directly or indirectly at centrally prescribed prices eg, to state organisations or on the regular retail market.

We may, for example, look at the manufacture of shoes. Taking the basic free market case, the cooperative would perhaps buy leather at R 70 per square meter and the realistic retail market (black market) price of a pair of shoes would be around R 200. On the other hand if the cooperative were able to buy leather through *Gossnab* at the unrealistically low controlled price of, say, R 15 the retail price would be controlled and would perhaps be about R 40, thus preventing the cooperative from making an exorbitant profit.

It should be emphasised that cooperatives are under no obligation to enter into special agreements with the state. Article 19 merely covers cases where it does enter into an agreement eg, for the purchase of raw materials, and its provisions are aimed at preventing unjust profits at the consumer's expense.

In the event of an excess profit being made it must be forfeited to the state budget and an additional fine in the same amount is imposed.

Distribution of profits and taxation of income

These two items are dealt with in Articles 20 and 21 of the Law on Cooperation. The distribution (or perhaps 'application' is a more suitable word because dividends as such are not mentioned in this article but in Article 22 which will be discussed below) of profits of cooperatives was another widely debated matter. Those siding with 'forced levelling' ie, equal salaries all round without regard for the type of labour involved (not to be confused with 'parity' which relates to equal rights) attempted to impose very high tax rates which would have rendered it impossible for a member of a cooperative legally to earn more than about R 500 per month. However common sense prevailed.

In the first of the two articles, the legislator set out what are only general guidelines to the cooperatives as to how they should apply their income from sales: they may apply it in paying for materials required for meeting production and financing costs and in paying for labour and social benefits. Again, state intervention in connection with application and use of income and formation of reserve funds is strictly out of bounds. Indeed, all these matters are in the exclusive authority of the general meeting of the cooperative.

So a cooperative may pay any salary it wishes to its employees and, as we shall now see, no real damage will be caused by the applicable income tax rates. The practical result of all this is that cooperative employees earn salaries that, on average, are about 70 per cent higher than state salaries.

At the time of the debate on the Law on Cooperation there already existed the Decree of the Presidium of the Supreme Soviet dated 14 March 1988. This Decree imposed progressive rates of tax on the profits of cooperatives of up to 90 per cent, but public opinion prevailed and the Decree was not put into effect. Cooperatives were therefore, initally, entitled to continue enjoying their previous privileged tax rates whereby their profits were taxed at 2–3 per cent during the first year of operation, 3–5 per cent during the second year and up to only 10 per cent after the third year. However, this has been changed and the various republics now impose tax at varying rates depending on the type of activity being carried on by the cooperative. For example, the RSFSR passed a decree on 6 June 1989 whereby some of the tax rates are as follows:

Type of activity	Percentage tax
Care for children, disabled persons etc.	3
Agricultural produce	10
Consumer goods production for children and the elderly	20
Construction works, research and development	25
Public food services	40
Agency and middlemen	60

Taxation of monthly salaries is also progressive and in 1990 will probably be as follows:

Roubles	Percentage
100	8
101-700	13
701-1000	20-25
1001-1500	30-40
1501 +	up to 50

A further 6 per cent is added in each case where the tax payer is childless.

Because of the far-reaching tax benefits, a practice has developed whereby the local councils of deputies in the cooperative's local area of activity has been able to benefit from the cooperative's business. In the course of the changes that have been occurring in the USSR, more power has been devolved to these councils and the cooperative sector has been allocating part of its revenues and services for their benefit. Contributions may be made, for example, for the purpose of social and economic development of the particular area. Cooperatives even tend to include in their statutes, as one of their objects, an undertaking to assist in the solving of a particular local problem by allocating part of their profit to the council or to carry out certain works free of charge. This may smack of illegality to western ears (or noses) but it is all open and above board, the object being to benefit the parties involved mutually. The pay-off for the cooperative may be, for example, allocation of better offices or even lower taxes.

Financing, insurance and shares

A cooperative is free to use its financial resources which comprise revenues from sales, depreciation funds, individual and collective contributions, bank loans and money raised on the issue or shares, as it sees fit without outside interference.

A cooperative is entitled (but not obliged) to insure its property. At present the choice is between the state insurer *(Gosstrakh)* and the state cooperative, *Tsentroreserve*. However, cooperatives have the right to set up independent insurance brokerages.

Article 22, which refers to finance and insurance, also deals with the issue of shares. These would not be like ordinary shares or ordinary stock but would be closer to preference shares, or even debentures, and are merely a means for raising capital without granting the holder the right to vote at the general meeting. The article sets various ground rules, the most significant of which are as follows:

1 The shares are secured by the total property of the cooperative (hence the similarity to debentures).
2 The overall value of the shares must not, as a rule, exceed gross income of the cooperative for one year (presumably the last financial year preceding the issue of the shares).
3 The nominal value of the shares and the procedure for paying dividends is set by the general meeting, for the entire life span of the shares. The general meeting may however amend the dividend procedure, from time to time.

The permit for the issue of the shares is granted by the relevant financial body, subject to the consent of the bank which finances the cooperative's activities, after the necessary research has been carried out. There is a right of appeal to a higher financial body against a refusal to grant such a permit.

Once again, there is, in this article, a disclaimer by the state in relation to liability for obligations made by the cooperatives in connection with the share issue.

The right to issue shares is also available to federations of cooperatives.

Banking

Article 23, which has as its title the partial misnomer 'Credits and Accounts', actually deals almost entirely with the banking rights of cooperatives with regard both to where they should do their own banking and, more interestingly, to the opening of their own banks.

The article starts out by stating that newly created cooperatives may be given credit on favourable terms as determined by the relevant bank, for the purpose of setting up business. The observant reader will have noticed that this is an apparent instruction to state banks to come to the assistance of the new phenomenon of the Soviet economy.

A cooperative may open accounts in various branches of the bank to facilitate operations between its head office, branches, sales and service outlets and agents. The choice of the bank is left to the individual cooperative, subject to the proviso that each cooperative may operate with only one current account for local currency and another for foreign currency. A cooperative is not permitted to withdraw cash except to pay wages. At present cooperatives generally hold some cash independently of the bank and make quite substantial payments in that form, but this practice is disappearing. Indeed, Article 23 provides that the cooperative will determine how much cash will be available from time to time for its routine operations.

The article also gives specific authority to a cooperative to apply its own financial resources to extend credit to other bodies. Furthermore, cooperative federations have the right to create independent cooperative banks covering either a particular business sector or a specific territory. The first, *Soyuz-Bank*, was set up in Chimkent (Uzbek SSR) in August 1988. Cooperative banks have also been set up in Moscow, Leningrad and other locations.

Although Article 23 provides that such banks will be set up to provide resources for cooperatives, they have also been active in financing operations of state organisations and even deal with individuals. Their start up capital is normally about R 50,000,000 (£50,000,000 according to the official exhange rate or about £2.5 million if the black market rate is applied) and they normally offer better terms than state banks.

When asked to compare cooperative banks and state banks, Soviet businessmen have been known to say that when you go into a state bank you are asked to give so many details and answer so many questions that before the interview is finished you realise that you do not deserve a loan! Cooperative banks tend to be more understanding and listen to the client's problems. They are also authorised to be active in matters related to the issue and redemption of cooperative shares and payment of dividends. They may also invest their own funds in cooperative activities eg, as venture capital.

Employment conditions

Article 25 regulates general conditions of employment and terms of payment for labour. Subject to the general rule that terms of employment of cooperative employees should not be worse than state employees, the cooperative is fairly free to fix its own terms. In practice, these are far better than for state employees. Payment may be in money or kind and there is no limit on the maximum salary.

Employees may be members of the cooperative or non members and the cooperative may be their primary or secondary place of work. The local council of deputies will determine the ratio of members vis-à-vis non members to be employed, but the number of members must predominate and in practice the number of non members employed is agreed with the local council of deputies. Article 25 expressly states that employees for whom work at the cooperative is a second job are free from the normal formalities ie, the special notice and references, which are sometimes difficult to obtain (see 'Membership of Cooperative') relating to people who wish to work in two places, and that their pensions, study grants and salary at their main place of employment are not to be adversely affected.

Non members will be employed under an individual contract signed by the chairman of the cooperative. These contracts reflect the existing legislative norms of labour relations of the USSR and the relevant union republic but will incorporate the special provisions reflected in the cooperative's statutes. Article 25 sets out a list of items that are to be determined by the statutes ie, the length of the working day and hours of work, when holidays will be granted and for how long. Thus a considerable amount of freedom is extended to the members to determine the conditions of employment.

The same article also obliges the cooperative to make social security deductions to be paid to the state national insurance fund at the rates determined from time to time. At present the rate is 7 per cent of the salary but it may be increased to 15 per cent.

Article 24 directs that the cooperative should assist its members in housing eg, by providing loans, and that special consideration should be shown to war and labour veterans. The cooperatives may even construct housing and educational facilities for its members.

Raw materials and material-technical support

Unlike state enterprises, cooperatives are free to acquire raw and semi finished materials, tools and equipment and any other item required for production from any source. These sources may be roughly divided as follows:

* in the wholesale trade, from state organisations and enterprises and cooperatives;

* from collective farm markets;

* in the retail trade from state organisations and enterprises and cooperatives;

* from other suppliers by agreement.

Local councils of deputies are entitled to draw up blacklists of items of certain goods which are not to be sold to cooperatives in the wholesale market. If a cooperative is producing goods under state tender it must have materials and supplies made available to it from centrally allocated sources. There is another aspect to the sale of production materials by state enterprises: the state-owned wholesaler, *Gossnab*, has attempted to corner the market in certain items eg, polymers, leather skins and paper, in order to maintain high prices on sales to cooperatives, who are prepared to pay these prices because they can pass on the cost to the consumer. Article 24 also mentions the cooperative's entitlement to purchase or lease, from any source, unused buildings, machinery, equipment and means of transport.

Foreign economic activity

The inclusion in the Law on Cooperation of the provisions set out in its Article 28 was one of the more notable achievements of the protagonists of radical economic reform in the USSR.

The question of foreign economic activity may be broadly divided into two areas: foreign trade and creation of joint ventures in one form or another. The article grants cooperatives what amounts to a carte blanche in these fields. In the realm of overseas transactions are included regular export and import transactions which may be carried out directly by the cooperative or under contract with state foreign trade organisations. Foreign currency earned in export transactions goes to the cooperative subject to a deduction of between 30-60 per cent which is paid to the state against roubles at the official exchange rate. If the exporter is a federation, the foreign currency remaining will be divided between the cooperatives relative to their contribution to the particular transaction. These funds may then be applied in importing equipment, raw and semi-finished materials etc. for use in developing production and enhancing turnover. If the export transaction is carried out through a state foreign trade organisation the payments will made to the state, and the cooperative's foreign currency account at *Vnesheconombank* will be credited with its share.

Joint ventures may be set up by cooperatives (the word 'federation' is not mentioned in this context) with *Comecon*, western (the Law says 'capitalist') and third world countries. This aspect will be developed in the discussion on joint ventures.

The state and cooperatives

The state is obligated by Article 29 of the Law on Cooperation to guarantee the observance of the rights and lawful interests of cooperatives and their members, including the basic right to form cooperatives. This is strong talk in a business law.

State bodies must provide assistance to the development and strengthening of the economic independence of cooperatives and to the growth of the effectiveness of their operations, while not permitting any limitation on the legitimate creative activity and initiative of members.

Specific forms of assistance to be provided by local councils of deputies and other state bodies are defined in Article 30 of the Law. These are:

• provision of land, production and other premises and equipment, either free or against payment of rent;

• assistance in improvement of equipment and techniques;

• advertising of the cooperative's produce, goods or services;

• assistance in formulation of economically efficient production structure;

• granting of various benefits.

The Soviet government runs management schools where new subjects such as marketing are taught. In return for meeting the costs of courses, cooperative members are entitled to be trained at such schools on an equal footing with employees of state enterprises and organisations. At the same time, article 31 promotes state assistance in the establishment, by cooperatives and federations, of their own independent vocational and technical institutions and schools, training centres, refresher courses and other types of centres aimed at teaching technology and design, scientific research and planning. Cooperatives are also permitted to send their members abroad for training.

The relationship between the state and cooperatives in matters of bookkeeping, accounts and audit is governed by article 32. A cooperative must keep proper books of account and statistical records in accordance with state rules. Auditing is performed by the cooperative's internal auditing commission or by that of the federation to which the cooperative is affiliated and financial statements are sent to the local financial authorities which deal with taxation.

Types of cooperative

The Law on Cooperation divides cooperatives into three broad categories: collective farms and agricultural cooperatives; producer and service cooperatives; consumer cooperatives. We will deal briefly only with the second and third types.

Most of what has been said in this chapter has related to producer and service cooperatives but we feel that the reader may wish to note the principal areas where consumer cooperatives differ from producer cooperatives. But first, a word on the basis characteristics of consumer cooperatives. Article 45 of the Law on Cooperation defines their major functions as follows:

1 The creation and development of retail networks and public catering organisations.
2 The supply of food and other goods to members and the population in general and coordinating on this with state trade enterprises and organisations.
3 The purchase of agricultural produce and raw materials, manufactured goods and other products from individuals and collective and state farms, for processing and marketing through the retail market and supply to the industrial sector.

Members of consumer cooperatives have priority in purchase of goods sold in cooperative stores and in sale of their produce (from their own fields or workshops) through the consumer cooperative network of procurement and trade groups. Other cooperatives eg, producers, and organisations and enterprises may join a consumer cooperative.

The specific provisions of the Law on Cooperation relating to production and service cooperatives are contained in Articles 40–44, from which the main points to be noted are that the right to membership of producer cooperatives depends on an employment contract and preference will be given to persons who will be employed in work related to the basic production activity. Article 40 prohibits the private employment of people where the objective is not related to the establishment and operation of a co-operative.

On the other hand, membership of a consumer cooperative

(also known as consumer societies) does not depend on the employment of a member by the cooperative. The only prerequisite for membership is payment of a membership fee and regular dues. Obviously, only a person interested in taking advantage of the marketing and distribution services provided by the cooperative would be interested in joining.

As we stated earlier, the liability of producer cooperative members is not limited and they are liable for the debts to the extent provided in the statutes. On the other hand the liability of a member of a consumer cooperative for its debts is limited to the amount of his subscription fee.

After liquidation of a producer cooperative its assets would be realised and any surplus, after payment of debts, would be distributed to its members in accordance with the statutes. On liquidation of a consumer cooperative, however, any surplus would be paid to the federation to which the cooperative belonged.

Conclusion

The creation of cooperatives with the full backing of the state has provided enterprising people of the Soviet Union with an outlet for their energies. Entrepreneurs' and citizens' economic independence has been legalised within a reasonably stable organisational framework. The very fast growth rate of the cooperative movement seems to justify the government's decision to introduce the new vehicle which has been incorporated into the economic life of the country on a virtually equal footing with other economic bodies.

As the political system gradually moves away from its communist ideology it must be presumed that the private sector will go from strength to strength. It is not inconceivable that further changes will be introduced into the Law on Cooperation to bring cooperatives more into line with the private and public limited companies of the west.

However, there are, at the time of writing, no drastic changes on the agenda and the prevailing condition is likely to remain intact for the next year or so.

Having dealt with the apparatus available to the local population we will now turn to the means devised by the USSR to attract foreign investment and assistance in pulling its colossal and cumbersome economy into the twenty-first century.

4

Setting up a joint venture

Background

If 1 July 1988 was a red letter day for the private entrepreneur in the Soviet Union, 13 January 1987 was no less significant for the foreign investor who wished to try his luck in this huge new market.

On that date the Presidium of the USSR Supreme Soviet published a decree 'On Questions Concerning the Establishment in the Territory of the USSR and Operation of Joint Ventures, International Amalgamations and Organisations on the Territory of the Soviet Union with the Participation of Soviet and Foreign Organisations, Firms and Management Bodies'.

Fast on the heels of the above decree came decree no. 49 of the USSR Council of Ministers, also dated 13 January 1987 and entitled 'On the Establishment in the Territory of the USSR and Operation of Joint Ventures with the Participation of Soviet Organisations and Firms from Capitalist and Developing Countries'.

This latter decree, which will serve as the basis for our discussion on joint ventures will be referred to simply as 'the Joint Venture Law'. We will, however, almost invariably use the terminology adopted by the official translator whose work appears in Appendix 2.

The reader will have noticed that the decree refers specifically to 'Capitalist and Developing Countries'. On the same date the Council of Ministers passed a parallel decree covering joint ventures with members of *Comecon*. We will, however, devote our attention to Decree no. 49.

The objectives of the Joint Venture Law are succinctly summarised in Article 3 where official bodies are exhorted to set up joint ventures in order '. . . to satisfy more fully the domestic requirements in certain types of manufactured products, raw materials and foodstuffs, to attract advanced foreign equipment and technologies, management experience and additional material and financial resources into the USSR national economy, to expand the national export sector and to reduce superfluous imports'.

Here was a country, one of the two world superpowers, that had opened up space to mankind and sent the first man into orbit round the earth, admitting that it could not produce a decent hamburger. Such a statement, despite its flippancy, should not be ignored any more than natural human instincts that it reflects. It was not by chance that the McDonalds chain chose Moscow as the site for their largest outlet, capable of accommodating 700 customers at any one time.

There is, of course, more to Decree no. 49 than the consumer's appetite for fast food. The basic infrastructure of the Soviet economy was paralysed. It had been realised that capitalism was not all rotten and the best way to introduce the better facets of the previously despised and denigrated system was for Soviet organisations to enter into partnership with capitalist businesses. There was an opportunity for the Soviet economy to absorb the latest technology and equipment (although the United States is only slowly and grudgingly showing an inclination to withdraw its stringent restrictions on advanced technological exports to the Soviet Union), to organise efficient production and distribution systems, to upgrade the quality of goods and to enhance their export potential. That, at least, is the theory and it is feasible that after the passage of several years the objectives of the exercise will be achieved. It will, however, be a slow process.

International joint ventures are by no means a Soviet invention. The People's Republic of China adopted the vehicle of equity joint ventures to encourage foreign investment as long ago as 1978 and, inasmuch as it has been able to attract many well known companies to invest there through this vehicle, it has been successful. The factor common to the PRC joint venture and the Soviet one is that they are, in themselves, legal entities. In comparison, if an English company and USA corporation were to set up a joint venture in the United Kingdom it is more than likely that they would form a third company as an independent entity to serve as the operating vehicle for the venture. In the Soviet Union the joint venture itself will be the 'company' and the partners' liability will, as we shall see, be limited.

The main characteristics of joint ventures are:

1 The bringing together of the capital resources of the partners under one roof in various forms such as the injection of cash or the supply of equipment.
2 Joint management.
3 Mutual enjoyment of profit and mutual responsibility for losses subject, of course, to the rules relating to limited liability.

The advantages of such an arrangement to the Soviet partner are clear and do not require any amplification, but why would a western company want to take its hard earned money and invest it in an obviously undeveloped market, particularly at a time of so much political risk? Suffice it to say that a potential market of nearly 300 million people cannot be dismissed lightly and there are sometimes advantages to be had by getting in on the ground floor. To these must be added the existence of cheap labour which may be combined with western technology to produce goods at a price that will be attractive to both the local Soviet market and to export markets throughout the world.

The Joint Venture Law attempts to define the rights and obligations of the parties to the joint venture while taking into account the special features which are aimed at attracting foreign investment, such as reduced tax rates, repatriation of profits in freely convertible foreign currency, limitation of liability of investors, absence of state interference in the operations of the joint venture and freedom to operate in local and export markets, without directives from above, subject to the qualification that if the Soviet partner is a state enterprise the achievement of state objectives may sometimes have to be taken into consideration.

Having regard for the fact that even an experienced legislative body such as the British parliament does not always manage to get the desired results it is not surprising that steps have already been taken to amend some of the original provisions of the Joint Venture Law and the main ones are contained in the decrees set out in Appendices 3 and 4. These will be discussed in detail below, but for foreign investors the most important points are that the original provisions limiting the foreign partner's share in the joint venture to 49 per cent and the requirement that the chair and director general (the equivalent of managing director or chief executive officer) of the concern both be a Soviet citizen, were both repealed.

Somewhat ironically, the activities of many joint ventures do indirectly (and sometimes even directly) assist in fulfilling state plans. One of the original major motives that encouraged the introduction of the joint venture conception was to broaden the export basis of the USSR, so it is quite common to see in the internal statutes of joint ventures, where the Soviet partner is a state enterprise, that the joint venture will be the sole vehicle for the exports of that partner. But that partner itself is still very much a part of the state and its central planning and, therefore, in performing the export functions of that partner, the joint venture will be executing state plans. This will not be true, of course, where the Soviet partner is a cooperative, unless the cooperative itself is owned mainly by a state entity. It should nevertheless be remembered that there is another side to the coin of partnership in a joint venture with a state enterprise and that is that raw materials will be more readily available. This particular imbalance may redress itself as the cooperative gradually asserts itself as a viable alternative to state enterprises.

Having dwelt for a while on general principles we will now enter into a discussion on the specific provisions of the Joint Venture Law to be followed by a detailed examination of a typical joint venture agreement between Soviet and foreign partners and the internal statutes of the joint venture itself which, we hope, will assist in clarifying some of the practical matters that will be faced by the potential investor in a Soviet joint venture.

The joint venture law

Legal entity

Possibly the most important provision in the Joint Venture Law is contained in Article 6 which states that 'Joint ventures are legal entities under Soviet law'. In order to leave no doubt as to the meaning of this, the article then sets out a list of legal acts that may be performed by a joint venture including entering into contracts, acquiring proprietary and non-proprietary rights and suing and being sued. The article adds that the ventures created under this law shall be self financing, self supporting and shall operate on the basis of full cost accounting – another revolution for the Soviet Union.

To this must be added the limitation of liability provisions of Article 18. It will be recalled that production cooperative members do not enjoy this privilege, at least not on paper. The powers that be obviously took into account that foreign investors would not readily take chances in the uncharted territory of Soviet free enterprise without being afforded some protection in return for their considerable risk. To emphasise the novelty of the law, the Soviet Union also granted itself immunity from liability for the obligations of the joint venture. On a more practical note, mutual protection was granted to affiliates of joint ventures against liability for the joint venture's obligations and vice versa.

Establishment of a joint venture

Article 2 of The Joint Venture Law, as amended by Decrees nos. 1074 and 1405 of the USSR Council of Ministries dated 17 September 1987 and the 2 December 1988 respectively, requires the Soviet partner to submit the proposal for the establishment of the joint venture ie, the agreement between the parties (accompanied by a feasibility study and draft statutes) to one of several bodies, depending on the location and personality of the Soviet partner.

The law as originally drafted only took account of the possibility that the Soviet partner would be a state, or state related, organisation and provided that the application be sent to the ministry or government agency under which it operated. Decree 1074 decentralised the application procedure by including among the offices to which the application could be sent, the councils of

ministers of union republics. Decree 1405 amended this provision still further to allow for cases where the Soviet partner is an
independent cooperative (the decree actually only refers to producer cooperatives so it is clear that the legislator does not envisage
the setting up of a joint venture with a consumer cooperative). In
such a case the independent cooperative has the option to send
the application, in addition to the offices referred to above and
depending on the location of the cooperative, to the city councils
of Moscow or Leningrad or to an area or regional council.

The filing of the application is, of course, the culmination of a
long process which can take many months or even years. We will
now look at the preregistration scenario which is not dealt with in
the Joint Venture Law.

Preliminary stage

Joint ventures are created under many different circumstances
and it would be impossible, within the scope of this book to cover
them all. We will therefore refer to a hypothetical case where a
western company has had regular trade contacts with a Soviet
manufacturer and is now investigating the possibility of setting up
a partnership with its Soviet counterpart with the object of selling
the produce of the venture both in the internal market and by
way of export.

Once the partner has been found the parties should carry out
preliminary research on, and address their attention to, the following matters (where necessary the name of the official Soviet
body that should be approached is added in parenthesis):

1 Possibilities of selling joint venture's products on internal and
   foreign markets having regard for the price that the product
   could command (Soviet foreign trade organisations).
2 World prices for raw materials.
3 The cost of equipment.
4 Loan facilities that would be available from Soviet banks in
   hard currency (*Vnesheconombank*), in roubles (*Zhilsotsbank*)
   and for construction costs (*Promstroibank*).
5 The availability of raw materials and equipment etc. in the

Soviet Union (USSR *Gosplan*, *Gossnab*, Ministries and other suppliers).
6 Factory construction costs and conditions (USSR *Gosstroi* in local areas and Ministries of USSR construction enterprise).
7 Preparation of business plan.
8 Drafting of agreement, statutory documents and preparation of feasibility study for establishment of joint venture.

One of the subjects that will almost certainly be brought up by the Soviet partner is the transfer of technology to the joint venture. As we shall see, special provisions have been included in the Joint Venture Law which emphasise the Soviet Union's protection of patent rights. The statutes of the new entity will set out the agreement between the parties on this matter to which we will refer in rather more detail later.

A decision as to whether to use local or imported equipment will have to be made, depending on the results of the research carried out by the parties. Equipment is available in the USSR but it might prove more advantageous to import more up to date equipment from elsewhere, even though the initial cost may be higher.

Once all the preliminary research has been carried out the parties should then attempt to reach a modus vivendi which should be based broadly on the following items:

1 Pricing and organisation of sale of products on home and overseas markets.
2 The amount of start-up capital required. The Soviet legislator actually adopted the term 'Authorised Fund' which is likely to cause some confusion to lawyers conversant with English company law where the expression 'authorised capital' is used to define the total amount of a company's share capital, issued and unissued, and is not necessarily related to the real value of the company at any one time. In this book we will adopt the Soviet legislator's use of the expression which will, therefore, cover the total original investment in the joint venture (and any subsequent investments) and will include the value of equipment introduced to the venture by the respective parties,

the cost of original raw material acquisition and cost of other material and technical resources (including any cost for transfer of technology) and construction costs (except for those costs that are covered by loans). In evaluating equipment, buildings, infrastructure and other tangible assets that are introduced to the venture by a party but which are not actually acquired from a third party, account will be taken of world price levels, a factor that is likely to work in favour of the Soviet party and must be carefully monitored by the foreign investor. Likewise, the level of rental payments for land or water supply or mineral or other natural resources which may be put at the disposal of the venture by the Soviet partner must all be evaluated in accordance with the 'Rules for Evaluating Land, Natural Resources, Building and Construction, Provided by the Soviet Participants as their Contribution to the Value of the Authorised Fund of the Joint Venture Provided for Temporary Usage by the Joint Venture Conditions of Lease', approved on 30 June 1987. On the basis of these costs and of any other contributions of the parties to the start-up costs, their shares in the authorised fund of the joint venture will be cal-culated.

3 The credit requirements of the joint venture in local and foreign currency and the likelihood of there being available income to service the resulting debit. Loans may be required in foreign currency for the purpose of importing machinery from abroad and long term rouble credits may be necessary to cover construction costs of industrial buildings or for development of the material-technical basis of the plant and the human-social sphere which could cover such fields as construction for the residential and educational needs of the workforce. When examining these aspects reference may be made to the 'Rules For Lending to and Repayment by Joint Ventures, International Organisations and Firms of Capitalist and Developing Countries' which were approved by *Gosbank* and *Vnesheconombank* and were published in September 1987 (see Appendix 5).

4 Transport costs for supply to the intended location of the joint venture's plant of raw materials and equipment.

5 The supply of scientific-technical documentation and organisational and production manuals in Russian.

6 The life expectancy of the joint venture, the possibility of
extending the joint venture beyond that period and the expectations of the parties in the event of liquidation.

7 The extent to which the respective opinions of the parties are
going to carry weight in the management of the joint venture
and any special compensation that should be made available to
the foreign partner for its special contribution to the joint
venture in the areas of the economics and organisation of production.

Before moving on to the feasibility study and in order not to
create the impression that the Soviet joint venture may be
formed by only two parties, there are some that have been
formed by three or more partners. It could, for example, be of
great advantage to a proposed joint venture between say, an independent cooperative and a western firm, to bring in a state
enterprise as a third party in order to eg, enhance the supply of
raw materials to the joint venture. It may only be necessary to
give such a body a minimal holding of say, 1 per cent in return for
the facility of maintaining supply.

Feasibility study

The Joint Venture Law lays down no guidelines for the contents
of the feasibility study which is one of the documents that have to
accompany the application for registration. Therefore some flexi-
bility is possible but the following suggestions are proposed as an
outline for such a document.

The study should commence with a general description of the
proposed joint venture, its major objectives, identification of the
partners, the proposed location, the proposed initial authorised
fund, the supply of raw materials and equipment that will be
required for production and their sources of supply, conditions of
material-technical support required and where it is proposed to
obtain this, the potential markets for the sale of the products, the
proposed source of labour supply, details of the financial standing

of the proposed foreign partner and a statement as to the necessity, if any, to finance the establishment and current operations of the venture by loans.

The next section should describe the economic justification for the establishment of the joint venture between these particular parties in the specified location with special emphasis being placed on the advantages of the operation of the joint venture for the economy of the Soviet Union in general and for the region where the enterprise is to be established, in particular.

These items should then be followed by a detailed study of the joint venture that should, at least, cover the following items:

Capital financing

This should include such matters as the required start-up capital and how this is intended to be constituted, the amount of working capital that is likely to be required on an annual basis, the capital requirements for possible future expansion and planned expenditure on research and development.

Authorised fund

The items to be covered should include the total initial contribution of each of the respective partners, the structure of the initial capital, the proposed timetable for advancing the initial capital and guarantees that are to be provided to secure the advance of the capital as agreed between the parties.

Market details

This section should note the intended markets for the products, the projected levels of sales in each market, forecast of market trends in the future, likely sources of competition and proposed marketing methods to be adopted by the joint venture and the reasons for choosing such methods.

Equipment and machinery

Here there should be detailed lists of the machinery and equipment that would be required to commence production, setting out each item with its technical description, the name of its manufacturer, its year of manufacture and its cost or (if it is used) its market value.

Labour requirements

Details should be given on the number of employees likely to be required, over a period of years including their breakdown into administrative, production and skilled and unskilled categories. If the required labour force is not available in the intended location solutions to this problem should be set out.

Loans

There should be details of loans required by the joint venture, the probable terms of repayment (period of repayment and interest rates), the collateral and guarantees to be made available to the joint venture and the funds that it is expected will be available from income to service the loans. As regards foreign currency loans to be obtained from foreign banks, their repayment will normally be guaranteed by *Vnesheconombank* which in turn will seek collateral such as the undertaking of the joint venture to cover the debt supported by eg, written commitments from potential purchasers of the venture's products, to purchase certain quantities.

Income and expenditure

Projected income and expenditure statements for the first three or four years' production should be prepared and attached to the feasibility study. These will of necessity be of a speculative nature but are a sine qua non of the paper.

It should be emphasised that the above list cannot serve as a hard and fast rule and is by no means exhaustive. Each case should be addressed in an individual way. We have merely intended to convey to the reader a general picture of the type of document that the Soviet authorities would like to see.

Registration

Upon the issuing of the approval for the establishment of the joint venture by the relevant body eg, the council of ministers or individual ministry of a union republic or Moscow city council, the statues (or 'foundation documents' as they are defined in Article 8 of the Joint Venture Law) as approved, will be signed by the parties whereupon they come into force. Unfortunately this does not mean that the gestation period of the joint venture is complete. There still remains the stage of registration with the USSR Ministry of Finance.

Article 9 of the Joint Venture Law provides that the joint venture will acquire the rights of a legal entity at the time of registration. The grounds for refusal to register are that the submitted documents do not conform with the legal codes of the USSR, on the establishment and operation of joint ventures in the USSR, but the likelihood of rejection is minimal having regard for the fact that the documents will already have been under the scrutiny of the approving body and the only probable ground for refusal to register would be technical eg, because of incorrect completion of a form.

The requirements for registration are contained in Instruction no. 224 of the USSR Ministry of Finance (Minfin) of 24 November 1987 entitled 'On the Rules of Registration of Joint Ventures, International Unions and Organisations, Established on the Territory of the USSR with the Participation of Soviet and Foreign Organisations, Firms and Management Bodies'.

Parts 4 and 5 of the Instruction provide that the written application for registration of the joint venture shall be submitted (for approval) by one of the participants in the joint venture (for purely practical reasons, this will be the Soviet partner) to the Department of State Revenue of the USSR Minfin. The application must be accompanied by notarised copies of the statutory documents, a copy of the decision of the approving body (republican council of ministers, city council etc.), a notarised copy of the certificate of incorporation of the foreign party (assuming it to be a company) and a bank reference. This list does not preclude the possibility of the registration body requesting production of further documents. Any subsequent changes must also be duly reported to the Department of State Revenues.

This body will notify the auditing organ of the Minfin (Inaudit) of the registration of the joint venture and a notice of registration to the joint venture's office. This will also be published in the press.

The following documents and information will be entered on the joint venture registry at the Minfin:

- a joint application for the registration of a joint venture;

- the agreement between the parties and the statutes of the joint venture;

- the approval of the council of ministers (or other approving body) authorising establishment of the joint venture;

- brief description of the foreign partner (certificate of incorporation, by-laws, bank references etc.).

Agreement and statutes

The agreement between the parties is as close a document to a regular commercial agreement for the establishment of a joint venture as one could hope for, having regard for the fact that it is being reached with a body that is just entering the age of legal enlightenment. It does have some Soviet idiosyncrasies, some of which may be observed in the joint venture agreement set out in Appendix 8 where, it is hoped, the reader may observe the type of document he or she may sign at some future date. At this point we will restrict ourselves to a list of items that should be covered in the agreement and which, in fact, could serve as a general guide for preparation of a Heads of Agreement which might be entered into between the parties after completing their preliminary discussions (although some of the points would be superfluous in such a preliminary document). The items are as follows:

1 The parties.
2 The intended name and location of the joint venture.
3 A declaration that the joint venture will be one that will accord with Soviet law from the moment of registration.
4 The aims and objects of the joint venture.
5 The rights and obligations of the joint venture as a legal entity.

6 The rules governing transfer of the interest of one of the partners to an outside party.

7 The extent of the initial authorised fund.

8 The share of each party in the initial authorised fund and the
structure of their respective investments.

9 Timetable for the injection of capital investment in the joint
venture.

10 Composition of the management and financial organs of the
joint venture.

11 Voting procedures and percentage majorities in particular
cases.

12 Material-technical supply to the venture and sale and marketing of its products.

13 Rules for transfer of intellectual property rights to joint venture and protection of those rights.

14 Issues of taxation.

15 Distribution of profits including transfer abroad of part due to
foreign partner.

16 Rules for covering possible losses and further investment by
the parties.

17 Legal standing of personnel and other matters relating to
employees.

18 The period for which the joint venture is to be established
together with option to extend this period.

19 Settlement of disputes between the parties.

We will now turn to the statutes of the joint venture for which
article 7 of the Joint Venture Law both provides a list of contents
and gives an option to the parties to 'incorporate other provisions
related to the specific character of joint venture's operations
unless they are contrary to Soviet law'. This leaves considerable
inventive power to the parties in a country where the norms of
private companies are virtually undiscovered territory. It is not
inconceivable that the inventiveness of drafters of statutes may
one day find their way into Soviet normative laws.

The statutes, which have to be formally approved by the
parties either simultaneously with the signing of the agreement or

at the first general meeting, must contain the following mandatory points:

- the nature of the joint venture;

- the objectives of its operations;

- its legal address;

- the list of partners;

- the amount of the authorised fund;

- the shares of the partners therein;

- the procedure for raising the authorised fund (including foreign currency content);

- the structure, composition and competence of the venture's management bodies;

- the decision-making procedure and the issues to be unanimously settled;

- the joint venture liquidation procedure.

Property of the joint venture and contribution to the authorised fund

Article 11 of the Joint Venture Law sets out the property that may form the basis of the parties' contributions to the authorised fund including buildings, structures, equipment and other assets, the right to *use* land, water and other natural resources, buildings, structures and equipment, as well as other proprietary rights (including the right to work inventions and use know-how), money assets in the currencies of the partners' countries and in freely convertible currencies.

It will be noted that although buildings and structures (or the right to use them) may be contributed to the joint venture, only the right to use land, water and other natural resources may be included in the conveyed property. The reason for this is that, while a building may be owned by the contributing party it could not, under present Soviet law own the land itself because all the country's land, mineral wealth, water resources and forests belong exclusively to the state. However, under Article 4 of the Decree of the USSR Supreme Soviet of 13 January (which immediately preceded the passing of the Joint Venture Law by the USSR Council of Ministers) land etc may be alloted to joint ventures either free or against payment all depending on the degree of importance that the joint venture has for the economy of the country. Payment for, eg, water resources will be calculated in advance for the whole life expectancy of the joint venture and will be paid for by the Soviet partner. The amount of the payment will be determined by a special committee of the local council of people's deputies.

The right of the joint venture itself to own, use and dispose of property is guaranteed by Article 15 of the Joint Venture Law, provided that this is done for the objectives of the joint venture's activities. This property may not be requisitioned or confiscated in administrative proceedings. Such a provision serves to underline the weight that the Soviet authorities wish to give to joint ventures. This protection does not, however, extend to regular execution proceedings following a judgement against the joint venture by a competent judicial authority.

It should be borne in mind that once the parties have transferred property to the joint venture as part of their contributions to the authorised fund this becomes the exclusive property of the joint venture itself: the quid pro of this is, of course, that the partner receives the right to share in the profits of the venture and also to a share of the assets in the event of liquidation. These provisions do not apply to property in respect of which only rights of possession and/or usage are granted: in such a case the value of such property will not be taken into consideration in calculating the partner's share in the authorised fund as it will remain the property of that partner.

Article 13 of the Joint Venture Law provides that 'equipment, materials and other property imported into the USSR *by the foreign partners* in a joint venture *as their contribution to the*

authorised fund of the venture are exempt from customs duties'
(authors' emphasis). The above words have been emphasised not
merely because of their obvious importance in calculating the
start up costs but also to compare their comparatively limited
application with the wide extension of this exempt status privilege which was introduced by Decree 1405 of 2 December 1988.
By this Decree, goods imported to the USSR *by the joint venture* itself for the purpose of *expanding production* may be totally
exempt from or subject to only minimal customs duties.

The property of the joint venture must be insured with the
USSR insurance agency – Ingosstrakh and the rules of insurance
are contained in USSR Minfin Instruction no. 45–15–1 of 5 June
1987.

We will complete this section with a discussion on the evaluation
of the respective contributions of the partners which is dealt with
by Article 12 of the Joint Venture Law. The value of the Soviet
partner's contribution is evaluated (in roubles) on the basis of an
agreed price that will be determined 'with due regard' to world
market prices. The same world market price provision applies to
the foreign partner's contribution. However an additional
requirement puts this partner at a certain disadvantage vis-à-vis
its Soviet counterpart ie, that the value of its contribution be converted to roubles at the official exchange rate as on the date of the
agreement between the parties or on such other date as the
parties may agree. With the official exchange rate standing at £1
= R1 this makes nonsense of the calculations. This is because a
realistic exchange rate is closer to £1 = R10 (the exchange rate
applicable to tourists. It might even be more true to say that the
rate is even more favourable than this if the black market rate is
taken as the measure). Therefore if, for example the contributions are made totally in cash and the Soviet partner invests
R1,000,000, the foreign partner will have to invest £1,000,000 to
achieve parity: this despite the fact that, in real terms, its share is
worth ten times that of its counterpart. Care therefore has to be
taken in calculating values to ensure that this anomalous situation
does not deprive the foreign investor of his just share of the pie. It
would also be advisable to guard against any future change in the

official rate by including a relevant provision in the joint venture agreement.

The question may be asked, 'How, for example, is a building in the USSR, where there is no free market in the western sense, to be valued?' The answer is that where no market value is available in the USSR, the parties must look to values in the home country of the foreign investor. This could be another bone of contention in negotiations between the parties and must be dealt with carefully so as not to lead to an unjust result.

Finally, in this section, we will look at the shares of the partners. Article 5 of the Joint Venture Law originally prevented a foreign partner from receiving a share greater than 49 per cent of the authorised fund enterprise. In recognition of the dissatisfaction of foreign investors with this provision, an amendment was introduced by Decree 1405 whereby the shares of the parties fund shall be as agreed between them. The original authorised fund may, during the course of the life of the joint venture, be increased either by applying profits in additional investments or through additional contributions by the partners. In the latter case the shares may have to be adjusted to take account of the additional investment and it is important to make sure that the statutes cover such an eventuality.

Transferring a share in a joint venture to a third party

This right is set out in Article 16 of the Joint Venture Law which permits the transfer of all or part of a partner's share in a joint venture to a third party subject to 'common consent', which presumably means 'with the consent of the other partner or partners'. The Soviet partners are given a right of first refusal to acquire the shares of the foreign partners but the corresponding right is not available to foreign partners. Any transfer must be endorsed by the State Foreign Economic Commission of the USSR Council of Ministers. It is not clear whether this means the 'approval' or if the intention is to 'rubber stamp' approval although one must assume, that if the identity of the third party did not conform with expectations of the commission, such endorsement would not be forthcoming. In any event it would be wise to cover the question of transfer of shares very carefully in the agreement and statutes.

5

Operation of joint ventures

Management organs

Article 21 of the Joint Venture Law (as amended by Decree 1405) governs the question of the management of the joint venture. 'Governs' is perhaps too strong a word because of the brevity of the provisions of the article which give some leeway to the participants in the venture to decide certain procedures for themselves.

The directives contained in the law are as follows:

1 The governing body of the joint venture is a Board consisting of persons appointed by the partners.
2 The Board's decision making procedure is defined by the foundation documents.
3 The operational activities are governed by a Management consisting of Soviet and foreign citizens.
4 Principal questions regarding the activities of the joint venture are resolved at board meetings on the basis of unanimity.
5 The chairperson (in using this expression rather than the official translator's 'chairman' we have deferred to modern western usage) of the board and the director-general may be foreign citizens.

The last two provisions were introduced by Decree 1405 and the decision to allow either or both of the two senior functionaries to be foreigners represents an important concession by the Soviet authorities and serves to underline their strong desire (bordering on desperation) to attract modern managers to reform the country's beleaguered economy.

A typical set of statutes will determine the following matters: the number of board members divided into representatives of the respective parties in proportion to their holdings in the authorised fund; the term of a board member's period of office; the appointment of alternative board members to attend meetings in the absence of another member; the member's right to resign; the filling of vacancies on the board; the appointment of the chairperson and director-general; the date for convening the annual general meeting and the matters to be discussed there and the matters in respect of which a unanimous decision is required which will most likely include:

- matters of general policy, long-term plans, changes in range of products, research and development budget, the annual budget and deviations from it;

- amendment of statutes;

- reduction or increase of the authorised fund;

- transfer of share of a partner, in whole or in part, to a third party;

- change in percentage share of any partner;

- admission of new partner;

- merger with another legal entity;

- sale of principal business or of whole or part of the fixed assets;

- change of objectives;

- substantial changes in the structure of the joint venture by eg, establishment, acquisition, sale or dissolution of a subsidiary or affiliate;

- liquidation of the joint venture;

- election of director-general and deputies;

- board regulations;

- approval of balance sheet and profit and loss account;

- establishment of reserve and other funds;

- *non*-distribution of all or part of distributable profit;

- approval of changes in the organisation of the joint venture and in the size of the work-force and transfer and dismissal of senior staff;

- acquisition, leasing or disposal of immovable property;
- contracts between the joint venture and any of its partners;
- agreements with trade unions;
- acquisition, disposal or licensing of patents, trademarks, or other intellectual property;
- conclusion, amendment or termination of agency and other agreements;
- taking out or granting loans over a certain amount for a medium or long term;
- all transactions in excess of a specified amount;
- initiation of legal proceedings or concluding settlements in respect of a sum exceeding a certain minimum limit.

At first glance the above list seems to contain some items that would be best left to a majority, rather than unanimous, decision and its final contents would depend on the parties' interpretation of the requirement, in Decree 1405, that all matters of principle be determined by unanimous decision. A comparison of statutes of joint ventures registered prior to the passing of Decree 1405 with those of the post-1405 era will reveal that the list of items requiring a unanimous decision in statutes of the latter period tends to be much longer. It seems that the policy of drafters of statutes is 'better safe than sorry'!

The statutes will also set out the procedure to be adopted by the board and will cover such aspects as the quorum for meetings, the number of votes that each board member is entitled to (which is generally one although there is no reason why there should not be weighted voting in certain circumstances), the times and pretexts for convening board meetings, the notice that has to be given of board meetings, who has the right to convene board meetings, the venue for meetings, whether voting may be by means of fax etc. and the language in which the minutes shall be kept (normally in Russian and English).

The day to day affairs of the joint venture will be handled by the management which will probably comprise the director-general, his deputies and the chief accountant, and will be directly responsible to the boards. The director-general is the key figure and his functions will include, within the general framework of carrying out the board's directions, organising the activities of the joint venture and implementing the board's decisions, concluding agreements in the name of the enterprise where this does not require the special approval of the board, representing the board before third parties including state bodies, supervising the preparation of periodical reports and financial statements for the board, handling all the financial affairs of the joint venture including its relationships with banks, appointing and dismissing non senior staff on an individual basis and defining their duties, terms of employment and salaries within the limits of the board's guidelines and making other day to day decisions which are not within the prerogative of the board.

Business of the joint venture

Freedom of activity and foreign trade

Article 23 of the Joint Venture Law guarantees the independence of joint ventures to develop their own business without the interference of state bodies which shall neither '. . . fix mandatory plans for a joint venture nor. . . guarantee the sale of its products'. There are, however, certain fields which are forbidden territory for joint ventures ie, the manufacture and maintenance of military equipment, munitions etc, mining and refining gold and precious metals (this does not preclude dealing in gold coins and there is at least one joint venture operating in that area) and the production of narcotics.

Until the advent of the Joint Venture Law, the right to carry on import and export trade to and from the Soviet Union had been the exclusive privilege of the Ministry of Foreign Trade (now merged in the new Ministry for Foreign Economic Relations) which executed its business with its numerous foreign trade missions set up throughout the world. These missions and other state-run organisations still exist but some dramatic changes have been introduced in the past three years. One of these appears in Article 24 of the Joint Venture Law which permits joint ventures to carry on independent import and export transactions (including with the Comecon countries). The joint venture is free to choose whether it wishes to avail itself of the services of the official trade bodies or not, but is not obliged to do so.

Some of the joint ventures formed in the early days after the law was passed exploited this provision to make a quick profit. This was achieved by their acting as middlemen in transactions where the principals were buying up cheap surplus state produced goods at a very low price and disposing of them overseas at enormous mark-ups.

Partly in order to overcome this problem but principally both to open up and regulate foreign trade in this new era the USSR Council of Ministers passed Decree no. 203 of 7 March 1988, which came into force on the following 1st April. The principal provisions of this decree are as follows:

- its provisions apply to all bodies 'participating in foreign economic relations' whether state owned or otherwise;

- all types of foreign activity are covered including, 'direct production and scientific-technical relations, coastal and cross border trade and barter operations';

- a registration system has been established whereby any entity wishing to carry on foreign trade must register with the USSR Ministry of Foreign Economic Relations or with its local representative office;

- the ministry is required to set up a centralised and computerised data system covering all registered participants in foreign trade;

- there is a specific provision obliging all those bodies which had a right to participate freely in foreign economic relationships, prior to the introduction of the decree, to register also (this being a clear reference to joint ventures);

- the ministry was empowered to make enquiries with many bodies, including banks, to verify data included in the registration applications;

- a system of compulsory customs cargo declarations was established detailing all cross border transactions whether carried out independently or by state bodies – the information contained in these declarations now serves state statistics gathering;

- joint ventures may only export the goods (and works and services) they produce themselves or import goods (and works and services) that they require for their own needs and a special permit is now required from the State for any joint venture (or indeed a producer or cooperative) to 'conduct intermediary operations';

- a general power is granted to the state foreign economic commission of the USSR Council of Ministers to limit import/ export activities or suspend the operations of participants in foreign economic relations for certain periods of time or in relation to specific products or to a particular state or group of states, for the purposes of controlling demand and supply on the local market, effecting international obligations of the USSR in relation to import/export controls, achieving mutually beneficial agreements at international trade negotiations and taking corresponding measures against discriminatory acts of foreign governments. (These provisions do *not* apply to the export of products of joint ventures or to imports required for their own use;)

- there is a similar power to suspend in the event of 'unfair competition' or 'activities (that) prejudice the interests of the state'. An example of 'unfair competition' is dumping while a complete list of the 'prejudicial' activities appears in article 10 of the decree (see Appendix 3).

There is nothing really Draconian in the above regulations which exist, in one form or another, in the legislation of 'capitalist' countries. The USSR merely found it necessary to enact them in order to adapt itself to the new conditions it had created. As long as all foreign trade was state-run no special regulations were required. The fact that they were introduced nearly one year after the right to trade freely was granted to joint ventures serves to underline the inexperience of the Soviet legislature in free market matters. There will, no doubt, be many more cases of shutting the stable door after the horse has bolted.

Communications

The last paragraph of Article 24 of the Joint Venture Law blandly states that, 'A joint venture is entitled to maintain correspondence, as well as telegraph, teletype and telephone communications with organisations in other countries'. That is the theory, but anyone who has tried to contact someone in the Soviet Union by telephone during normal business hours will look upon the words of the law with incredulity, to say the least.

The state of communications in the Soviet Union is nothing short of catastrophic. At present it is virtually impossible to obtain a direct dialling line for telephoning abroad and that, of course, includes lines for fax machines. The postal service is slow and erratic – letters do usually reach their destination, later rather than sooner! Fax messages will be received if the lines are free but it is better to despatch them after the population in the particular area in the Soviet Union have gone to bed! Most overseas calls from the Soviet Union have to be booked in advance and it has been known for the contact to be made several days later! The best means of communication to and from the USSR is telex, provided your Soviet counterpart has been able to obtain one. There is, however, light at the end of the tunnel, because the British telecommunications firm GEC–Plessey has entered into a joint venture in the USSR with the objective of revamping the whole system and it would appear that improvement is on its way. The only concrete result, so far, has been the installation of the credit card telephone in the USSR, the first one having been hooked up at the Savoy Hotel in Moscow, but some more far-reaching improvements are expected in the near future.

Foreign currency payments and receipts

Article 25 of the Joint Venture Law provides that, 'All foreign currency expenditure of a joint venture, including transfer of profits and other sums due to the foreign partners and specialists shall be covered by proceeds from sales of the joint venture's products on foreign markets'. On the face of it this article appears to say that no payments may be made by the joint venture in foreign currency unless they are covered by equivalent receipts in such currency. This would be particularly worrying for the foreign investor in connection with the vexed question of repatriation of profits which is normally among the first matters broached by a person making initial enquiries about a foreign investment.

However, Article 32 states quite categorically that, 'Foreign partners in a joint venture are guaranteed that amounts due to them as their share in distributed profits of the joint venture are transferable abroad in foreign currency'. This is, indeed, an example of bad drafting by a hurried legislator who became obliged to reconsider the question. If the example of Mcdonalds is considered it is clear that this particular joint venture would be unlikely to generate any income in sales 'on foreign markets' but it is equally improbable that companies of the stature of McDonalds (or, for that matter any other company) would enter into such a venture if it did not believe that it will one day be able to repatriate its profits in foreign currency.

Finally we must consider the contents of Article 26 of the law, as originally enacted. Its provisions required that the joint venture's local sales of its products and its local purchases of equipment, raw and other materials, components, fuel, energy and other produce be '. . . paid in roubles on the basis of contractual prices with due regard for world prices'. A quasi solution was found in Decree no. 352 of the USSR Council of Ministers of 17 March 1988 which amended Article 26 to the effect that both sales of goods by the joint venture and the purchase of equipment etc. on the internal market would be effected in such currency as may be agreed between the parties in each particular case. Here indeed is active encouragement to enter into transactions in the Soviet Union in foreign currency.

Material-technical supplies

One of the major problems facing a production joint venture is finding sources of supply to fulfil its demand for raw and other materials and equipment. As an example of the practical difficulties involved there may be related the true story of a European shirt manufacturer who wished to set up a joint venture in one of the union republics. The negotiations had reached a very advanced stage and all the major problems, such as allocation of land and buildings and finding the labour source had all been solved. The foreign partner then told the Soviet counterpart which different colours of shirt material would be required for the first year of production. The shirts were to be striped in an assortment of different colours. The Soviet partner enquired and ascertained that for the first year the only colour stripe available was blue and in consequence of this limitation the whole transaction came to an abrupt halt.

There are basically two sources of supply in the Soviet Union ie, the wholesale market and the state distribution system. The wholesale market has developed as a result of the existence of surpluses that have been accumulated by enterprises that have either overproduced or that have been produced by a manufacturer in accordance with production targets and who has then been advised that *Gossnab* has decided, for some reason or another, not to distribute these products. The wholesale market has been developed by *Gossnab* in different centres throughout the Soviet Union. There is a central listing of the goods available at any one time together with the demands received from various sources. *Gossnab*, in consideration of a commission, matches the demand with the supply. Volumes are relatively small but this is the closest phenomenon in the Soviet Union to a wholesale market and the authorities hope that, with the growth of joint ventures and cooperatives a non state market will develop. The shirt manufacturer referred to above could, perhaps, in order to have overcome his problem, have considered the possibility of establishing its own textile plant to manufacture shirt material both for himself and for export.

Banks and credit facilities

The provisions of Articles 27–29 of the Joint Venture Law set out the general principles forming the basis of the relationships between joint ventures and the banks. These may be summarised as follows:

1 Credit facilities may be made available to joint ventures on commercial terms in foreign currency either at the *Vnesheconombank* or, with that bank's approval, at foreign banks which will probably request a guarantee from *Vnesheconombank*. Rouble facilities may be obtained either from the *Vnesheconombank* or from other state banks;
2 The *Gosbank* and the *Vnesheconombank* have a right to examine credit facilities granted to joint ventures to ensure that they are being applied for the right purposes;
3 The joint venture's money is deposited with *Gosbank* if it is in roubles, and at the *Vnesheconombank* if it is in foreign currency. Interest will be earned on the above accounts at world market rates on foreign currency and at local rates on roubles (about 3–4 per cent);
4 Fluctuations in exchange rates of foreign currency (presumably as against the rouble) deposited in a joint venture's account shall be carried to the joint venture's profit and loss account. (The inclusion of this provision in an article dealing with bank customer relationships is another example of inexperienced drafting).

A rouble account will be opened at the nearest local branch of *Gosbank* to the joint venture's head office while the foreign currency account will be opened either at the head office of *Vnesheconombank* or at a local branch if there is one nearby. Credit will be advanced on terms no less favourable than those enjoyed by state organisations under the Rules for Crediting Material Reserves and Production Expenditure approved by *Gosbank* on 30 October 1987. In addition to the banks actually mentioned in the Joint Venture Law it is customary for joint ventures to obtain credit facilities from the USSR *Promstroibank* for the purposes of financing construction costs.

The decision on whether to grant facilities and for what amount will be determined on a yearly basis in accordance with plans presented to the bank by the joint venture (setting out the purpose for which the advance is required, the amount required, the period for which it is needed, the proposed terms of repayment, the collateral offered etc). The terms of credit may be revised from time to time in view of changes that may have occurred in eg, production conditions, raw material supplies or volume of sales. In the case of long-term credits for construction, expansion etc, the application will be more detailed and accompanied by additional documents such as extracts from the decision to approve the establishment of the joint venture, construction plans and details of the executors thereof, cost calculations, economic effectiveness calculations and the like.

Short-term credits in foreign currency may be made available to the joint venture in the event of a temporary shortfall of liquid funds, for the purpose of financing the purchase abroad of raw materials, spare parts and other goods required for production purposes. This right may be extended, where necessary, to cover the import of equipment, machinery and other major items for use in production. The bank will be secured by its right to attach and sell the machinery etc. in the event of default. Although there is not yet a Soviet system of pledge or charge the bank will have a security interest over a particular piece of machinery if it can show that the outstanding debt relates to an advance that was made for the specific purpose of acquiring that machine. If it cannot prove such a connection the machine will constitute part of the general assets of the joint venture available for all the creditors pro rata to the respective debts owed to them by the joint venture.

In the event of default by the joint venture where it has failed to pay amounts due in two consecutive months no new credits will be advanced. Provided that the debt is eventually repaid fresh advances may be made against improved collateral such as the guarantee of a foreign bank. Higher interest rates may also be imposed in the event of default.

Reserve and other funds

One of the sources that should be available for the partial settlement of the joint venture's debts is the reserve fund which it is obligated to establish under the provisions of Article 30 of the Joint Venture Law. The statutes of the enterprise will either fix or provide that the board will determine the amount of annual deductions to be made from profits and allocated to the reserve fund until the total of the fund reaches the equivalent of 25 per cent of the authorised fund. A typical example would be 10 per cent of profits to be paid in annually to the reserve fund until this reaches the prescribed 25 per cent.

Other funds may cover such items as production expansion, research and development, social development and material incentives for employees. The amounts to be allocated from profits for these funds would be determined by the board. On a different note, a depreciation fund would also be established under the terms of Article 33 of the Joint Venture Law in accordance with '. . . regulations applying to state-owned organisations unless a different system is stipulated by the foundation documents'. A joint venture might, for example, determine that the fund should be based on renovation trends existing in world markets bearing in mind the necessity of keeping up with high production standards. Alternatively, different percentage deductions may be applied to different items of property. There is a lot of scope for creative accounting in this particular area.

Distribution of profits

In accordance with Article 31 of the Joint Venture Law the profits of a joint venture, net after deduction of '. . . amounts to be attributed to the USSR national budget and sums allocated to form and replenish the joint venture's funds shall be distributed among the partners in proportion to each partner's share in the authorised fund'. This needs no explanation, except for the fact that the 'amounts to be attributed to the USSR national budget' means, principally, taxes. We have already dealt with the payment of the share of the profits due to the foreign partner in foreign currency.

Disputes

Article 20 of the Joint Venture Law provides that the USSR courts shall have jurisdiction in disputes between a joint venture and other Soviet organisations (including other joint ventures) and between the partners in a joint venture. The article also protects the right of any of the parties to such a dispute to settle their differences before an arbitration tribunal. It will have been noticed that disputes between the joint venture itself and any of its partners or between a joint venture and a foreign entity are not included in the above list and according to one source* it appears that in such cases only the courts will be entitled to try the case (*Sovmestiniye Predpriatya Mezhdunarodniye Obyedinenya i Organizatsii na Territorie SSSR* p 319 (*Yuridicheskaya Litteratura,* Moscow 1989)). It appears, however, that it would not be impossible for the parties to such a dispute to go to arbitration abroad if they both felt such a step to be in their best interests although there might be some difficulty in enforcing the arbitration award in the Soviet Union. It is common procedure for the parties to a joint venture to include an arbitration clause in their basic agreement for the establishment of the joint venture whereby they will attempt to settle all disputes between themselves by amicable negotiations or, if that path does not produce the desired results, by arbitration. Another point to remember is that, as has already been noted, a joint venture's property is immune from administrative justice and, therefore, an unpaid electricity bill, for example, would have to be persued in the courts. In the case of a Soviet consumer not paying such a bill, administrative execution could be levied without the necessity of court proceedings.

Taxation and staffing of joint ventures

Intellectual property rights and transfer of technology

The state of the Soviet Union's laws for the protection of intellectual property rights, particularly in the important field of patentable scientific inventions, is not all that could be desired. This is not due so much to the absence of adequate protection for registerable patents (such protection does exist and the Soviet Union is a signatory to important international conventions), but is rather a consequence of the weakness of the underlying political and economic system. A new patent law is, however on its way to the statute book having successfully passed its first reading.

Scientists, some of whom are now living close to the poverty line, will for the first time be entitled to obtain patent protection for their developments on an individual private basis. As a result of this they will then be able to sell their rights to the state and possibly to anyone else in the world. Under the present system it is simply not worth the scientists' while to go to the trouble and expense of registering a patent which would not augment their paltry state salary income in any way. There is a story of an enterprising Japanese man who would glean details of important new inventions which were published in great detail and on a regular basis in Soviet scientific magazines and then earn considerable amounts of money in his home country by selling the ideas.

In recognition of this rather sorry state of affairs a special provision was included in the Joint Venture Law (Article 17) whereby the intellectual property rights that belong to joint ventures are granted protection by Soviet Law '. . . including protection in the form of patents'. This will include both original technology produced by the joint venture and any intellectual property rights transferred to the joint venture by the partners. The licence for the transfer of technology by a partner to the joint venture and the method of their exploitation will be dealt with in the agreement between the parties and the statutes which may be supplemented by a licence and transfer of technology agreement. It should be noted that the Joint Venture Law actually talks of 'Industrial Property Rights' and does not adopt the word 'Intellectual'. We have decided, in this case, to ignore the official version which they consider inappropriate.

In the event of a transfer of technology to the joint venture by one of the partners, the estimated value thereof (including the value of royalties that would have been payable to the transferor by any other transferee) must be calculated and taken into consideration in evaluating the contributions of the partners to the authorised fund. This valuation could help to overcome some of the injustice caused by the necessity of calculating the hard currency investment of the foreign partner in accordance with the official exchange rate.

A joint venture will be entitled, in its own name, to patent its own inventions in other countries. This right is available to it under Article 105 of the Regulations on Discoveries, Inventions and Rationalisations Proposals which were approved by a USSR decree in August 1973.

Taxation, financial statements, accounts and audit

Taxation of the joint venture

Mark Twain once noted that the difference between a taxidermist and a tax collector is that a taxidermist takes only your skin. The USSR may not be exempted from this view. Despite the Soviet Union's desire to attract foreign investment it has so far been unable to find its way to granting really far reaching tax benefits to joint ventures. Certain concessions do exist but in comparison to those granted by eg, the Republic of Ireland they are quite miserable.

Article 36 sets the basic tax on the gross profit (called 'profit tax' and not 'income tax') of the joint venture, after allowing for deduction of payments to reserve and other funds 'intended for development of production, science and technology. . .' at 30 per cent. The initial sting is removed from this by a number of concessions which were subsequently introduced by Decrees 352 and 1405 the effect of which is that a joint venture will be exempt from tax on its profits for two years from the year in which it produces its first profits, inclusive of the first profitable year. (The original version of the Joint Venture Law limited this exemption to the first two years of operation only). In view of the fact that the law also provides for advanced tax payments on profits for a current year, based on assessments prepared in advance by the joint venture, the two year exemption actually results in deferral of tax payment for an additional year. This is simply due to the fact that the tax for the first profitable year will not be paid until the end of March in the following year, while no advance tax will have been paid unless, of course, the management of the joint venture had been so careless as to have prepared a profitable assessment for the year in question!

Two special benefits were introduced in relation to the fareastern economic region in order to stimulate investment there ie, the regular two year exemption period was extended to three years and the tax on profit was reduced to 20 per cent.

As stated above the Joint Venture Law includes provisions requiring advance tax payments to be made on the self-assessed profits of the current year. The provisions covering this point are contained in Article 37 which states that:

1 The amount of advance tax payment shall be determined by the joint venture itself on the basis of its financial plan for the current year. (It would appear that it would be quite legitimate for the new venture to prepare plans in its early years that show losses rather than profits. This strategy would have to be revised once the first profits have been made).
2 The final assessment to tax will be made on the 15th March following the end of the previous tax year (which will always be on 31 December).
3 Overpaid taxes may be set off against current advance tax pay-

ments or refunded (apparently without interest) at the request of the joint venture.

4 The amount of advance tax must be paid in four equal instalments on 15 of March, June, September and December in each current year.

5 A penalty of 0.05 per cent is payable for each day of delay in payment. This rule applies to all sums due, not only advance payments.

A right of appeal is available to a joint venture that wishes to challenge a tax assessment. The appeal is, however, to the same body that made the assessment although there is a further right to appeal to a 'superior financial authority' within one month of the ruling on the original appeal. The filing of an appeal does not suspend the payment of the tax.

Although the exemptions are granted by the Joint Venture Law a separate application must still be made to the local taxation authority which will forward the application to the USSR Ministry of Finance which will make the decision on whether the joint venture is entitled to the privileged status or not, within one month.

As a point of interest, it should be noted that the first profit of a joint venture formed under the Joint Venture Law was announced in January 1990. It was made in 1989 by a venture aptly called *Perestroika* which is a construction partnership between a Soviet organisation and United States' company.

There are two other types of tax on the joint venture apart from the profit tax ie, social insurance contributions (which will be discussed at a later stage) and charges for use of land and labour. A fixed annual tax (presently R600 per head) is payable in respect of each employee.

Taxation of distribution of profits

The Joint Venture Law, as originally drafted (article 41), imposed tax at the rate of 20 per cent, on that part of the profit of a joint venture that is due to the foreign partner and is transferred to it abroad. This meant that the total tax on that partner's share of the net profit of the joint venture totalled 44 per cent ie, 30 per cent profit tax and an additional 20 per cent on the remaining 70 per cent available for distribution (if distributed). This is not, to say the least, a very exciting proposition. It is true that double taxation treaties do exist between the USSR and other countries whereby tax on those distributions may be less than 20 per cent (in the case of the United Kingdom the rate is zero) and the original law does, in fact, refer to the application of the treaty provisions.

Here again change was subsequently introduced by Decree 1405 to the extent that it was necessary to recognise the fact that high tax rates were going to act as a deterrent against increased investment. The decree did not change the rate of tax but it did empower the USSR Ministry of Finance, from time to time, to lower the tax rate due on the foreign partner's share or even to exempt it totally from tax, unless this was contrary to any tax treaty between the USSR and the partner's country of origin. The decree indicated that this was particularly applicable in the cases of joint ventures active in the production of consumer goods, medical equipment, pharmaceuticals, high technology products having important domestic economic applications and also joint ventures in the far-eastern region.

Financial statements and auditing

These matters are dealt with in Articles 44–46 of the Joint Venture Law under the collective title 'Supervision of Joint Ventures' Operations'. The provisions of these articles set out the basic principles for: ensuring the rights of the partners to receive information about the enterprise's activities and financial affairs whenever they request this; bookkeeping; audit. The joint venture's statutes will contain the methods adopted for putting these provisions into effect.

In order to protect the partners' interests a typical set of statutes may provide that each partner has the right to receive information and make enquiries into any matter relating to the venture's operations and have access to the venture's papers and property of any kind and also, that the board and director-general shall provide any information required by a partner. There should be a provision in the statutes for the keeping of minutes of all meetings of the board and the management and that the minute books should be, at all times, available for inspection by the parties. It has been known for the statutes to provide that the meetings be recorded and that the tapes be stored.

Article 45 requires the joint venture to maintain operational, bookkeeping and statistical records in line with those used by state owned Soviet enterprises as specified by the USSR Ministry of Finance and Central Board of Statistics. It is not unusual, however, to find that the statutes will allow for the keeping of two sets of books, quite legitimately, the second set to accord with the law of the partner's home country. This would of course facilitate the incorporation of the joint venture's accounts in the partner's own financial statements. The venture's statutes would probably impose the responsibility for complying with the Soviet regulations (which by Article 45 is attributed to the joint venture) on its director-general and chief accountant. Article 45 also contains a stipulation that joint ventures shall not submit any accounting or business information to state or other authorities of foreign countries. With all due respect to the legislator it appears that this provision must have been included erroneously. Any public company, whose shares are traded on a stock exchange, that sets up a joint venture in the USSR, be it directly or through some subsidiary company, will be obliged to disclose such information in its annual reports, at the very least. The provision also runs counter to the spirit of double taxation treaties that provide for the exchange of information between taxation authorities.

The auditing of the financial, commercial and business activities of the joint venture is compulsorily (Article 46) carried out by the independent Soviet auditing organisation *Inaudit* but the statutes of the joint venture will almost certainly allow for the establishment of an internal auditing committee on which the partners will be represented. There are no such animals in the Soviet Union as chartered accountants or CPA's and the chief accountant of the joint venture will probably be a highly qualified university graduate in economics and statistics.

Personnel

Articles 47–51 of the Joint Venture Law set out the principles of employment of the enterprise's personnel. These are as follows:

1 Although both Soviet and foreign workers may be employed the majority must be Soviet citizens.
2 A trade union must be set up specifically for the joint venture and a collective agreement will be made between the two bodies.
3 The terms of the collective agreement must conform to the provisions of Soviet legislation and the statutes of the joint venture.
4 The basic working conditions of the Soviet employees will be governed by Soviet legislation which will also apply to foreign employees except in matters of pay, vacation and pensions which will be set out in the individual contract under which the services of these employees are retained.
5 The joint venture will make contributions to the state social insurance scheme in respect of all the employees, regardless of their nationality, and payments will also be made to state-sponsored pension schemes for all the Soviet employees. Pension contributions for the foreign employees may be transferred to their home countries in the currency of the respective fund.
6 Foreign employees salaries are subject to local income tax at the rate and in accordance with the procedure set out in the Decree of the Presidium of the USSR Supreme Soviet of the 12 May 1978 'On the Income Tax levied on Foreign Legal Persons and Physical Persons'. Any unspent part of the foreign employees salary may be transferred abroad in foreign currency.

We will now discuss some of the above principles in more detail, starting with the application of Soviet legislation (which derives principally from the constitution of the USSR, the Principles on the Law on Labour and the labour legislation of the union republics) to the employer-employee relationships in a joint venture and first, the question of remuneration. Soviet law imposes a minimum salary which is barely a subsistence wage. It is customary for joint ventures to pay its workers wages that exceed the average salary paid in the Soviet Union (about R 250 per month). The foreign employees will be paid far more than the Soviet employees and the bulk of their salary will be received in foreign currency.

The next aspect is the terms of work and rest. Here again the conditions must not be worse than the recognised minimum standards generally applicable in the country. This means an average working week of about 40 hours and a minimum annual vacation of 15 days (with a maximum of 24 days). Some classes of worker enjoy higher minimum standards eg, miners or other workers employed in hazardous or unhealthy conditions, or where there is a harsh climate or the area is remote, must not work more than 6 hours per day and are entitled to an additional 6–12 days paid vacation. Extra payment will be due for overtime or night work.

Salaries are usually paid in two halves eg, on 2 and 17 or 14 and 29 of each month. There are also provisions for the payment of reduced salaries during what are known euphemistically as 'waiting periods' ie, those periods when instructions come from above not to exceed production quotas. One would expect that, in a privately run business such as a joint venture, management will take steps to ensure that the work force is gainfully employed at all times.

A collective agreement will be concluded between the board of the joint venture and the trade union on behalf of the workers. The basis for this will be the customary agreement used in the Soviet Union to which the parties can add their own variations which must not, of course, lower the employees' conditions below the minimum standards referred to above. The agreement will cover the whole gamut of employer-employee relationships specially adapted to the requirements of the joint venture.

Design (planning) and capital construction

Article 34 of the Joint Venture Law sets out the basic principles governing the design (this is the word preferred by the Soviet translator of the law and although we believe that the word 'planning' is more appropriate we will defer to the translator) and construction of the joint venture's facilities, including those required for the social purposes of its employees. These principles are that the design and construction are the responsibility of the joint venture itself, both contractually and financially; that designs must be approved by the USSR State Planning Committee, and finally, that priority shall be afforded to joint venture construction contracts in regard to both the allocation of labour and the supply of materials.

The design and construction of industrial premises are, of course, subject to extensive regulation and these must be strictly adhered to. Failure to do so will result in the enforcement of administrative measures such as an order for the cessation of construction. The relationships between the parties involved at the planning stage ie, the joint venture, as client, the contractor and the planning authorities are governed by the Rules on Agreements for the Execution of Project and Research Works, approved by the USSR *Gosstroi*, USSR *Gosplan*, and USSR *Minfin* in 1959.

Prior to the final approval of the plans it will be necessary to obtain the approval of various bodies such as the Ministry of Energy, the local council of deputies and the (new) state committee on nature. According to a decree of the USSR Council of Ministers passed in 1979, each body is allowed, in theory, 15 days or, in 'special' cases, 30 days to discuss the documentation submitted to it.

The legal relationships between the joint venture and the construction organisation are governed by the relevant articles of general civil law codes of the respective union republics and by special laws such as those on the Rules of Agreements on Capital Construction Contracts adopted by the USSR Council of Ministers in 1986. The principles of these laws will be applied to joint venture constructions in the same way as they are resorted to when the client is the state although certain nuances are likely to be taken into account because of the special nature of the joint venture within the general framework of the Soviet economic system. Of particular note is the rule that the risk of accidental destruction of the building prior to its acceptance by the client is borne by the client. The joint venture will be able to insure against such an eventuality under an 'all risks' insurance policy to be taken out with *Ingosstrakh*.

Liquidation

Grounds for liquidation

A joint venture may be liquidated in accordance with the liquidation provisions set out in its statutes or by a decision of the USSR Council of Ministers in the event that it has been carrying on its activities in a manner contrary to the contents of the statutes.

Statutes do not normally set out a list of circumstances in which a joint venture should be liquidated. The normal provision merely states that the joint venture will be liquidated in accordance with the unanimous decision of the board.

The statutes will lay out the procedure to be followed after such a decision is made. A liquidation commission, comprising representatives of all the partners, will be set up whereupon the director-general will lose his or her authority. The joint venture's property will be disposed of and any property which the enterprise had been licensed to use will be restored to its owners. Any surplus, after payment of debts, will be distributed amongst the partners in accordance with their shares in the authorised fund. Article 52 of the Joint Venture Law provides that the foreign partner shall have the right to the return of its contribution in money or in kind, pro rata to the residual balance of the contribution at the time of liquidation going into force, after discharge of its obligations to the Soviet partners and third parties.

7

The future of joint ventures

Statistics

It is not always easy to rely on statistics to obtain a complete and accurate picture of any particular situation and this is no less true in relation to the available statistics on joint ventures in the USSR. This does not mean that nothing can be learned about joint ventures but it does mean that it is difficult to gauge the extent to which ventures that have been established under the Joint Venture Law are active and successful.

We can, however, ascertain some important data such as the types of industry that have attracted investors, their countries of origin, the amount of the authorised funds of the ventures and the areas in which they have been set up.

The figures available tell the story as at 31 October 1989. By that date 940 joint ventures had been established, although we would emphasise that certain data is available on only 933 (this number compares with 23 at the end of 1987, 168 at the end of 1988 and 749 at the end of September 1989, so it can be clearly seen that the growth rate has increased quite dramatically, from an average of 14 registrations per month in 1988 to a monthly average of over 94 by October 1989). Of the total, 748 (about 80 per cent) had partners from western countries and 105 (about 14 per cent) were formed with eastern bloc partners. Of the remaining 6 per cent, nearly all (60) are a partnership with an eastern bloc partner together with a country from the developing world.

The agreed initial authorised funds of these ventures totalled over 2.5 billion roubles of which the Soviet share amounted to 1.44 billion roubles (about 58 per cent) while western countries undertook to invest 862 million roubles (which was equivalent to over 1.4 billion US dollars calculated at the official exchange rate prevailing on the date the respective agreements were signed) representing 80.8 per cent of the foreign investment. Although this last figure tallies with the percentage of joint ventures in which the foreign partner is from the west, it does not reveal the size of individual investments.

The breakdown of the republics in which the joint ventures were established is as follows (data being available on only 933 operations):

Union Republic	Number
Azerbaidzhan	6
Armenia	9
Byelorussia	14
Estonia	60
Georgia	28
Kazakhstan	7
Kirgizia	–
Latvia	23
Lithuania	9
Moldavia	8
RSFSR*	706
Tadzhikistan	3
Turkmenia	–
Uzbekistan	7
Ukraine	53
Total	933

*Of these 478 were established in Moscow and 74 in Leningrad.

It is interesting to note that Estonia where the population only constitutes about 0.5 per cent of all-union population is where nearly 6.5 per cent of the ventures were established. The reason for this preponderance is the heavy involvement of Finland which has close ties with the Baltic states, particularly Estonia with which it shares a common cultural heritage.

The division into sectors is a little more complex. There are ten basic sectors and one of these, defined as 'Social Complex', meaning basically, services, is divided into seven sub-sectors:

Sector	Number
Fuel and energy	5
Metallurgy	5
Chemical/Timber	47
Machine production	40
Computer hardware & software production	122
Construction & building materials	60
Transport and communications	18
Agriculture	41
Social Complex*	308
Scientific design, consultancy, engineering, advertising, exhibition organising, agencies, personal education etc.	287
Total	**933**

*The sub-division of this sector is as follows:

Sub sector	Number
Trade	58
Tourism, hotel & transport services for the general public	53
Medicine, health care	46
Light industry	31
Consumer goods	58
Movie & video production, concert activities	37
Printing	53
Total	**308**

From the point of view of size, the bulk (58.1 per cent) had authorised funds of up to 1 million roubles, 27.2 per cent had funds of between 1 and 5 million roubles, 6.9 per cent required an initial investment of 5–10 million and the balance of 7.7 per cent were in the mega class of over 10 million roubles.

Finally, we come to the breakdown of the nationalities of the foreign partners. We will give the details of the western countries only and these include cases of joint investments with countries from the eastern bloc or the developing world:

Country	Number of investments
W Germany	138
Finland	110
USA	97
Austria	65
United Kingdom	65
Italy	61
Switzerland	48
Sweden	38
France	35
Canada	23
Japan	20
Netherlands	16
West Berlin	15
Spain	13
Liechtenstein	12
Australia	10
Belgium	9
Luxembourg	6
Greece	6
Norway	4
Ireland	3
New Zealand	3
Denmark	2
Total	799

Perhaps the two most surprising numbers are those relating to Finland, which accounts for nearly 14 per cent of the total (although this may not reflect the percentage of financial investment) and Liechtenstein! Of more importance are the figures relating to West Germany which, together with West Berlin, has partners in nearly 20 per cent of the established joint ventures while all the other Common Market countries between them account for only 26 per cent. Surprisingly, East Germany provided only one partner by October 1989. Of the eastern bloc countries, the most active were Bulgaria (28 partners), Poland (26), Hungary (22) and Yugoslavia (18). Among the developing countries, India with partners in 15 ventures far outstripped its nearest rivals.

Anticipated changes in joint venture law

Certain important changes in the Joint Venture Law are expected during the course of 1990 as follows:

1 The foreign participant could be an individual rather than a company.
2 Union republics may be given a more important role as to the regulation of the activities of joint ventures.
3 Regulations may be introduced regarding the minimum and maximum contributions of the foreign partner to the authorised fund.
4 The provision of bank references by the foreign partner may become compulsory.
5 Freedom of choice of auditors and insurance companies may be granted.
6 The joint venture may be permitted, upon the consent of the *Vnesheconombank*, to open foreign currency accounts abroad.

These changes have been mooted as a result of the discussions on the practical difficulties facing the joint venture under the present, rather restrictive, code and it is to be hoped that, as time passes by, the law will gradually evolve into a system that will become more accommodating to western investors.

8

General hints and guidance on doing business in the Soviet Union

We hope that the reader will now be armed with enough basic knowledge of the laws and technicalities that are going to affect the establishment of a business in the Soviet Union and now feel it appropriate to offer a few words of advice on how to make oneself feel as comfortable as possible both when negotiating the deal and in the après travail periods. As we indicated in the introduction to this book, this chapter cannot replace the excellent guide books that are available on the Soviet Union but we hope that our words will supplement the advice given there.

Visas, arriving in the country and accommodation

You will be unable to enter the Soviet Union unless you have first obtained a valid visa. If your visit is for business purposes you should ensure that your host sends you an invitation from his organisation. This should be directed to you (preferably by telex) and include your full name, date of birth, nationality, passport number and its date of issue. A parallel request ('visa support') should be sent to the visa section of your local Soviet consulate. It is not advisable to try to take out the visa yourself and the aid of an experienced travel agent should be sought. For a modest fee the agent will assist you in completing the visa application form which will be sent, with a photocopy of your passport, to the visa section. The application should be made not less than two weeks before your departure to ensure not being frustrated by bureaucratic delays.

Upon arrival at your destination (probably Shermetievo-2 Airport in Moscow) you will be faced by your first Soviet conundrum. You will possibly wish to use a trolley for your baggage and, in the probable event that you will not find a free one, you will have to pay for one, the price being one rouble. The laws of the Soviet Union prohibit the export of Soviet currency and you should, therefore, not have any. We cannot offer any legal solution to this problem and can only advise the traveller to use his wits!

You should ensure that your host meets you at the airport in order not to fall foul of the taxi service which we refer to below. Alternatively, the government tourist service, *Intourist*, arranges transport to the hotels and this may be prearranged.

Upon your arrival at the hotel (which may well be on the outskirts of Moscow – if that is where you are going) you will, after you have passed the truncheon-wielding policeman guarding the hotel from unwelcome intruders, check in at the reception desk. You will not complete a registration form but deliver your passport and visa to the receptionist who will hold it for about one day in order to enter you in the hotel registry and stamp the visa. You will be handed an hotel 'identity card' which will state your name (in Cyrillic script) and room number and must be carried by you at all times – without it you may not be able to enter the hotel or any of its restaurants.

You will then carry your own bags to your room and, upon entering it, you will probably ask yourself why you are paying so much money. The generally low standard (there are one or two notable and very expensive exceptions) of hotel accommodation in the Soviet Union is usually out of all proportion to its high cost. The bed may be narrow, the sheets may not be changed more than once a week, the towels may resemble dish cloths and you will get a tiny piece of soap which will only be replaced when it is almost invisible. It is a good idea to take your own towel and soap.

Eating in the hotel is unlikely to prove an exciting event and we would recommend that you try to restrict your gastronomic activities there to breakfast time (see our comments on restaurants below). If you like porridge you will be in luck because the Russian equivalent, known as *Kasha*, will be available in large quantities, together with black tea. This should give you plenty of energy to set out on your day's business!

There is normally no check out as such from Soviet hotels

because your bill will have been paid in advance and you are unlikely to be able to purchase any 'extras'. You can forget long distance telephone calls from the hotel. You will have a direct line in your room and you will be able to make free local calls. That, at least, is one benefit you may enjoy in the Soviet Union that is not normally available in the west.

Do not expect to be able to buy an English or American newspaper every day. You may find the *Herald Tribune* a day or two late but get up early! If you want to keep up with what is going on in the world take a good short wave radio so that you will be able to hear the BBC World Service. Otherwise you will have to survive on the English speaking broadcasts of Soviet state radio which tend to concentrate on local issues.

Customs, practice and procedure in business

Along with the advent of new business laws, the Soviet Union's first business school opened in 1988. You will discover that your Soviet counterpart is still at the bottom of the learning curve in such matters as protocol, office procedure and writing business letters. Having regard for the fact that the country has been ruled and regulated so stringently from the centre it may come as a surprise to discover that little or no direction has been given to government employees in the field of business protocol. The Ministry for Foreign Economic Relations, for example, does have a series of personal instructions for its employees but these are usually passed on by word of mouth. Examples of such instructions are, 'when in doubt wear English-style clothing' and, 'if you do not know how to eat a cake, eat an eclair'. Obviously a high standard of sophistication will take some time to achieve!

In such a deregulated situation a confusing atmosphere may arise in which a sense of freedom, on the part of your negotiating counterpart, may lead him/her into a feeling of insecurity. It is difficult to give any firm advice on how to handle such a situation except to say that you should act exactly as you would at home, subject to two important differences. First, make sure that you shake hands before and after every meeting and not only when you are first introduced. Second, always try to find out what the middle initial of your counterpart's name stands for. Every Soviet citizen's name is made up of three names: the forename, the patronym and the surname eg, Mikhail Sergeivitch Gorbachev, which literally means Michael son of Sergei Gorbachev. There is no title of Mr or Mrs in Russian and only a very close friend would use the forename alone. Therefore, your counterpart should be addressed as Mik*hail* Serge*i*vitch, Ivan Ivan*o*vitch (Ivan, son of Ivan) or *A*nna Pet*ro*vna (Anna, daughter of Peter) (we have indicated that part of each name that should be emphasised). This shows respect, will be appreciated and should lead to a more relaxed atmosphere which may be further enhanced by relating one or two well chosen anecdotes of which Soviet people are so fond.

The lack of business sophistication will probably manifest itself in the field of letter writing. It is unlikely that you will receive a letter from the Soviet Union in the commercial form to which you are accustomed. Your correspondent's epistle is likely to come in a form resembling an inter office memo without the trappings of a normal letter. For speed, the best method (apart from the expensive courier services) available for communication, as we have already stated (in course of the discussion on joint ventures), is telex and, with the anticipated improvement in the telephone system, the fax should become easier to use. Letters will take a long time arriving both to the office of destination and to the individual addressee because they will not only be delayed in the post but they will also have to be date-stamped, numbered, given a reply number, answered in writing and signed by someone in authority. Do not be surprised if you are asked to fax or telex the form of reply *you* would like to receive!

Making appointments, hospitality and entertaining

In their everyday lives Soviet people prefer not to plan well in advance and it is not easy to make business appointments far in advance. Most business appointments are made at very short notice, possibly on the spur of the moment. Even in the case of well known dates such as birthdays and public holidays it is customary to give invitations by word of mouth and with minimum warning. The concept of RSVP is unknown in the Soviet Union but there are possible alternatives to enable you to be fairly certain that a guest is going to arrive. If you send an invitation to the opening of a business exhibition, for example, it would be advisable to include words such as, 'After the reception, souvenirs will be distributed'. A souvenir may be one of a multitude of desirable (not necessarily expensive) gifts which may have little connection with the business event itself.

In arranging a meeting try to make it at as mutually a convenient a place as possible, taking transport or lack of it into consideration. We would not recommend the crowded metro as means of transport to important meetings although it is a sight to be visited as a tourist. Hopefully your host will have a Lada or Volga automobile and will be able to take you around or it may be a good idea to rent a car. Traffic is not that bad and you can park almost anywhere (there is a pleasant absence of parking meters and clamping is probably several years away). If you decide to travel by taxi try to avoid the black market drivers who will be crowding the entrance to your hotel. They will only want to take foreign currency and the deal you will have to negotiate will leave you with less money than if you hail an official taxi in the street (although even here you will probably have to bargain before you get in – it would be useful to be able to count from one to a hundred in Russian!) You might also learn the Cyrillic alphabet because all the street signs are in that script only.

As a general rule a traditional meeting is more acceptable than a working breakfast or lunch. Follow the normal practice of restricting the duration of the meeting and arrange for a written record to be made of decisions reached and the projection of future plans.

Dress for meetings as you would in your own country. Suits and ties are the general rule, particularly now that the television shows how neat and tidy Soviet parliamentarians have become. There is, of course, the problem of the weather in the Soviet Union and you will have to be well guarded against the cold in winter. The best advice is to cover yourself with layers that may be peeled off and left at the cloakroom. Be wary of thermal underwear though because all buildings are well heated and you might become uncomfortable in the oppressive heat. If, however, you are going touring, thermal underwear is a must in the heart of winter. Footwear should be sturdy with thick rubber soles which will not be destroyed by the salt that is sprayed on the road and pavement surfaces and will also grip better in ice than leather.

Occasions will arise when you will wish to entertain your Soviet counterparts. There are no black-tie parties in the Soviet Union and although there are evening receptions, cocktail parties are un-Russian. People prefer to sit down at tables rather than stroll about with a glass in their hand and if they are drinking they like to have something to eat also. Vodka is a throat rather than a palate drink – the quicker it goes down the better and there should be a good mouthful of food between drinks! A whisky and soda is regarded as a diluted drink and, therefore, a little wimpish. Gin may be mixed with fruit juice, including the popular mango or pineapple. Cognac is welcome at any time, be it before, during or after a meal and it is sometimes served with slices of lemon and icing sugar. One should not be surprised to see all the drinks on the table at the same time – vodka, brandy, red and white wine, champagne and any other alcoholic drink you may care to name, and also mineral water (in which the taste of the minerals may be very evident). All the wine will be at room temperature although you may have some ice to cool the white!

In southern parts of the country, such as Georgia, empty bottles will be left on the table as a reminder of how much has been consumed and in a restaurant you may be presented with a bottle of wine or champagne by people at another table, this being a sign of respect for foreigners. It would be correct to reply in a like manner, but the quantity should be doubled. But be careful – the doubling-up may continue until you will be in a state where you are unable to count the bottles!

Mealtimes in the Soviet Union are flexible. People may breakfast at home or when they arrive at work. Lunch breaks may be at any time between 11.45 am and 2.30 pm with just enough time for a sandwich at the firm's cafeteria, but some sit down as late as 4 pm and by then it is likely to be the main meal of the day. If you accept an invitation to a meal at 1 pm or later you may find yourself facing a very large meal. A business dinner after 6 pm may prove to be a real banquet with speeches and toasts and may be long and drawn out. On the other hand an evening invitation may prove to be in the realm of after dinner coffee rather than an evening meal so if you are feeling hungry it might be advisable to find out whether food is going to be served.

It is interesting to hear people who have never been to the Soviet Union talking about the terrible food that is served there. Certainly, in the past, it may have been true that finding good food was difficult (and even today the food in the hotels is not particularly appetising) but with the advent of the cooperative movement a large number of extremely good ethnic restaurants have sprung up in the big cities. You will be able to find almost any type of food from most parts of the Soviet Union, ranging from Georgian and Uzbeki restaurants to the better-known Jewish fare. It would be a good idea to invite your hosts to one of these restaurants but ask them to make the reservation (which sometimes have to be arranged well in advance). In this way the bill will be made out and payable in roubles which you will have exchanged at the advantageous tourist rate. A very good meal for four may cost about R 80, £80 according to the official exchange rate but, if you are able to pay in roubles, it will only cost you £8! Just remember not to speak English within earshot of the restaurateur! Also bear in mind that alcohol is not served at these restaurants although you may be able to take your own bottle.

Gifts

Any expensive present received by a Soviet business representative has to be handed into the protocol department of the organisation that employs them and will subsequently be shared. Such a gift may also be considered a bribe. Modest gifts like cigarettes, drinks, small bottles of perfume, a box of chocolates or books stand a better chance of being enjoyed by the person to whom they are given. If there is any hesitation over the acceptance of a gift or souvenir explain that is for the recipient's wife, husband, mother, father, children etc with a view to a coming event such as May Day, New Year, birthday, name day or whatever.

Women in business

At first sight it may appear that Soviet women still have to make their way into the business world. They are certainly few and far between in the trading organisations, but you will find that, as your contacts widen and you enter the realms of technological research, laboratories, exhibition organisation or production lines, they are there after all, particularly in the fields that they traditionally dominate, such as medicine and textiles. Here too it is worthwhile remembering the rules for addressing people by using the women's forenames and patronyms.

Public holidays

Public holidays cause a real hold up to any sequence of business negotiations and they make their presence felt all too long before they fall due. You will begin to notice people promising to do things 'after the holiday' and if you have to stay in the Soviet Union it will be just as well to have a proper break yourself.

The worst offenders are New Year, Soviet Army Day (23 February), International Women's Day (8 March), May Day (1 and 2 May), Victory Day (9 May), Constitution Day (7 October), and Revolution Day (7 and 8 November). Annual holidays are also the cause of considerable delays in proceedings, as the very specialist you need may depart for his vacation just as his superior, who has the final say, returns. In general, July may be bad and August even worse, but from 1 September the situation should improve.

The exchange of greetings and best wishes before holidays is expected and it may prove a good opportunity to present a small token of appreciation.

Currency

Your travel agent should have equipped you with two currency declarations, one of which is delivered to the customs on your arrival and the other on your departure. It should be evident from these forms how much foreign currency you brought in to the country and how much you are taking out with you.

The basic ground rule is only change the amount you think you will need. There should be an exchange office in your hotel where you may change foreign currency for roubles at the advantageous tourist rate. However, you will only be able to reconvert at the airport or one or two other specially appointed places and, if you are pressed for time or these offices are closed, you may find yourself with a lot of non-convertible roubles in your pocket. Remember that you are not legally permitted to remove Soviet currency from the country.

Credit cards are becoming more familiar and many items, from tourist services at *Intourist* offices to drinks in your hotel's hard currency bar, may be obtained with a credit card. Be aware, however, that the amount of the purchase is entered in roubles at the official rate at which your credit card account will be debited.

Conclusion

We have covered a few items which may assist you in acclimatising yourself to the business scene in the Soviet Union and we sincerely hope that these words will provide you with that little extra that is necessary when facing a new environment.

Good luck!

9

Stop press

As we stated in the introduction to this book, it has sometimes proved difficult to keep up with the pace of legislative change in the Soviet Union. Of the changes that have been introduced since the beginning of 1990 we have discussed, in some detail, the abrogation of the privileged position of the CPSU and the establishment of the new post of executive president. We have, however, made only fleeting reference to the new property law and no mention at all was made of the new land law. These two laws (particularly the property law), selected excerpts from which (in an unofficial translation that is believed to be the first to be published anywhere), appear in appendices 6 and 7, are so novel and tread such an unknown path that we decided to separate our discussion on them from the main text.

Both these new (and, as usual, hastily conceived and drafted) laws are to serve only as bases and their actual effect will only be felt after the introduction of many new all union and republican laws and, even then, it will be necessary to wait for some considerable time to ascertain if the people and the bureaucracy are able to cope with the new realities. We will now discuss the laws in brief.

The Law on Land

The Law on Land, passed on 28 February 1990 and which came into force two weeks later, commences with a statement of its general objectives which 'are directed towards rational usage and protection of lands, improvement of fertility of the soil, preservation and improvement of the natural environment and . . .' (probably the most significant of all) to provide '. . . equal opportunities for development of all forms of enterprise'.

The Law, which on close examination is not quite as revolutionary as one might have hoped, states quite categorically that every Soviet citizen has the right to a plot of land, subject to payment of land tax and to rules and conditions to be determined in subsequent legislation. The land will be 'provided' by the local Soviets who will also have the power to withdraw it (there are provisions for the protection of land occupied by minorities and ethnic groups). Apart from this power, the local councils will also be empowered, as indeed they already are, to allocate land for 'usage' and to lease land for specific purposes. The reader interested in knowing the purpose for which a right of usage (temporary or permanent) or for which a lease may be granted, is referred to Articles 6 and 7 of the Law in Appendix 7.

Probably the most revolutionary aspect of the new Land Law is contained in Article 5, which provides that Soviet citizens may acquire (be 'provided' with) ownership of land for life and that this right may be passed on to heirs. Under the previous law there was a limited system of 'ownership' – a short lease that could not be the subject of inheritance. Article 20 sets out the purpose for which such land may be provided which are: peasant farms (which may also be sold); personal agricultural use; for the building and maintaining of a residential dwelling; for gardening and the keeping of livestock; for a *dacha*; as an inheritance or the purchase of a house where any number of local handicrafts etc. may be carried on.

This new right of ownership is, however, more tenuous than it may first appear. First, it may not be disposed of on the open market – the land must first be withdrawn from its present 'owner' and then 'provided' to the new 'owner' (this does not apply in the case of a flat purchased in a state-owned block). Second, Article 9 of the Law lists the cases where the rights of usage and also ownership may be withdrawn (quite apart from the right of the council to compulsorily acquire the land for public purposes). These include the use of land for a purpose other than that for which it was provided. Therefore, it appears, that if someone is allocated land for residential purposes and he uses it for a business, that person may have the land confiscated. This would be understandable in the case of a lease or where a limited right of use has been granted, but it rather undermines the right of ownership which is shown to be apparent rather than real.

The Law on Property

At first glance this Law, which was passed on 6 March 1990 and came into force on 1 July, introduces some revolutionary concepts. It states, quite blandly (as though it is a fact of life in the USSR), that, 'The right of property in the USSR is recognised and protected by the law'. Then it provides that the property owner may own, use and dispose of the property that belongs to him (apologies to women but that is the wording of the law). The owner may conduct any lawful activity in relation to his property and the fruits of its economic use (unless otherwise envisaged by law or agreement – 'aye there's the rub') belong to the owner: this is the first mention in modern Soviet law of the possibility of profiting from the private use of property. Subject to laws that have yet to be enacted, the employment of hired labour for work in connection with the property will be permitted.

The property that may be owned is land (we have already seen the limitations imposed by the specific law which would, presumably, prevail), its resources, water, flora and fauna, buildings, structures, equipment, objects of material and spiritual nature, money, securities and other property (whatever that may be). Article 7 of the Law specifies, in greater detail, the types of property that may be owned by a Soviet citizen which are: residential houses, garden houses, dachas, plantations, means of transport, money, shares, other securities, personal objects, means of production for peasant and labour farming, personal farming, individual and other labour activity, and also the products of labour and profits therefrom. Private flats in state owned blocks may be purchased and disposed of freely.

There is quite a lot said in the Law on the various types of ownership, some of which are of particular significance to foreign residents. From reading the somewhat confusing Article 4, it appears that the forms of ownership and the persons who are entitled to own land are as follows: as regards Soviet nationals, ownership may be individual or collective and the Law also inevitably recognises state property; property may also be owned in the Soviet Union by foreign states, international organisations, foreign legal entities and foreign citizens (this presumably means that a foreign individual may also own a share in a joint venture which change is expected to be introduced to the Joint Venture Law also). Joint ownership by several persons and also by different entities, Soviet and foreign, is also permitted.

Special mention should be made of the rights of foreign citizens and legal entities. The latter may own, in the USSR, industrial and other enterprises, buildings, structures and other property for the purpose of conducting, through their use, economic and other activity – as envisaged by laws that have yet to be enacted. Provided these laws are enacted (or maybe even earlier, as a concession) this particular provision could lead to some interesting possibilities such as buying out state-owned Soviet enterprises. Foreign individuals are entitled to own property in the Soviet Union on the same basis as Soviet citizens subject to the exception that the principles applicable to peasant and other industrial activity will apply to them only if they are permanently resident in the country.

Most of the above provisions, as well as some others which we have not mentioned, are dependent for their effectiveness on the legislation of additional specific laws and regulations (which should ideally be introduced by 1991) without which they are likely to remain of academic interest.

At the time of going to press, yet another new law on 'share companies and limited liability companies' was published. This law adds to the list of legal entities now existing in the USSR and it is feasible that such a vehicle will be used by foreign investors.

Finally, from 1 July 1990, new bookkeeping and auditing regulations for joint ventures were adopted by the USSR Ministry of Finance. These are aimed (to the relief of western accountants) at aligning Soviet accounting methods with those prevailing abroad.

Appendix 1

The Law on Establishing the Position of President and Entering Amendments and Additions to the Constitution of the USSR was passed on 14 March 1990 and came into force immediately. The following is a summary of its important features.

I. Chapter 15(1) The President

The President is the head of the Soviet State. He may not be younger than 35 years old nor older than 65 (Gorbachev was 58 at the time of his election). He may not serve more than two terms of five years each. He is elected by the citizens of the USSR by secret ballot on the basis of universal, equal and direct elections, in which not less than one half of those entitled to vote participate. The candidate who receives more than 50 per cent of the votes cast throughout the Union and in more than half the union republics is elected. The first election was, as stated above, not carried out in this way.

The President is entitled to a salary only in respect of this post (and not e.g. as general secretary of the CPSU).

The President is the guarantor of the state's adherence to the constitution, of the laws and the rights and freedoms of the citizens. He protects the sovereignty of the USSR and the union republics and their territory and security. He also represents the USSR in domestic and international relationships.

If the above list is not enough, the President also performs the following functions:

- coordinates the highest bodies of state power and control;

- presents an annual 'State of the Nation' speech to the Congress of People's Deputies;

- presents candidates to the Congress for the posts of Prime Minister, Chairman of the Popular Control Committee, Chairman of the Supreme Court Procurator General and Chief

Arbitrator. He may demand the resignation of the holders of the above posts except (importantly, from the aspect of the separation of powers theory) the President of the Supreme Court;

- resolves, jointly with the Supreme Soviet, the questions of resignation or acceptance of resignation of the government;

- nominates and dismisses, in agreement with the Prime Minister, members of the government – subject to the subsequent approval of the Supreme Soviet;

- assents to the laws of the USSR and he has the right to return a bill to parliament for reconsideration, in which case a two-thirds majority will be required to enact it;

- is entitled to suspend the enforcement of a government decision;

- is the commander-in-chief of the armed forces and nominates and dismisses holders of senior military posts;

- conducts negotiations and signs international agreements;

- resolves questions relating to states of emergency in the USSR and to war;

- resolves differences between different sections of the Soviet parliament.

A presidential council is appointed by the President. This is a sort of think tank and may be viewed as an alternative to the Politburo. The Prime Minister must be a member of the council and the present council also includes the heads of the foreign ministry, the army, the KGB, the internal police and *Gosplan*. Only one member is not a party member.

The President may be removed by two-thirds majority of the members of Congress. In the event of his being incapable of fulfilling his activities, the President's powers are delegated to the Chairman of the Supreme Soviet and, in the event of his incapacity, to the Prime Minister. In such a situation a new president must be elected within three months.

Appendix 2

Decree (No. 49) of the USSR Council of Ministers (Official translation)

On the establishment in the Territory of the USSR and operation of joint ventures with the participation of Soviet organisations and firms from capitalist and developing countries.

For the purpose of further development of trade, economic, scientific and technical cooperation with capitalist and developing countries on a stable and mutually beneficial basis, the USSR Council of Ministers hereby decrees:

1. *General Provisions*

1. Joint ventures with the participation of Soviet organisations and firms from capitalist and developing countries ('joint ventures') shall be established in the territory of the USSR with the authorisation of the USSR Council of Ministers and on the basis of agreements concluded by partners therein.

Joint ventures shall be governed in their activities by the Decree of the Presidium of the USSR Supreme Soviet of January 13, 1987 ('On questions Concerning the Establishment in the Territory of the USSR and Operation of Joint Ventures, International Amalgamations and Organisations with the Participation of Soviet and Foreign Organisations, Firms and Managements Bodies'), by this Decree and other legislative acts of the Union of Soviet Socialist Republics and Union Republics with exceptions provided for by interstate and intergovernmental agreements, which the USSR is a party to.

2. Proposals in respect of the establishment of joint ventures with feasibility studies and draft foundation documents attached shall be submitted by Soviet organisations concerned to Ministries and government agencies, under which they operate. Ministries and government agencies of the Union Republics shall submit such proposals to the Councils of Ministers of their Republics.

The aforesaid Ministries and government agencies of the USSR and the Councils of Ministers of Union Republics shall agree upon the proposals with the USSR State Planning Committee, the USSR Ministry of Finance and other Ministries and government agencies concerned.

The agreed proposals for the establishment of joint ventures shall be submitted to the USSR Council of Ministers.

3. Ministries and government agencies, within the system of which Soviet partners in joint ventures operate, shall set up joint ventures with the purpose to satisfy more fully the domestic requirements in certain types of manufactured products, raw materials and foodstuffs, to attract advanced foreign equipment and technologies, management expertise and additional material and financial resources into the USSR national economy, to expand the national export sector and to reduce superfluous imports.

II. Partners in Property and Rights of Joint Ventures

4. One or more Soviet enterprises (amalgamations and other organisations) which are legal entities and one or more foreign firms (companies, corporations and other organisations) which are legal entities may be partners in a joint venture.

5. The share of the Soviet side in the authorised fund of a joint venture shall comprise not less than 51 per cent.

6. Joint ventures are legal entities under Soviet law. They may, in their own name, contract, acquire proprietary and non-proprietary personal rights, undertake obligations, sue and be sued in courts of justice and in arbitration tribunals. Joint ventures shall have independent balance [sic] and operate on the basis of full cost accounting, self-support and self-financing.

7. A joint venture shall have a statute approved by its partners. The statute shall specify the nature of the joint venture, the objectives of its operation, its legal address, the list of partners, the amount of the authorised fund, the shares of partners therein,

the procedure for raising the authorised fund (including foreign currency contents), the structure, composition and competence of the venture's management bodies, the decision-making procedure, the range of issues to be unanimously settled, and the joint venture liquidation procedure. The statute may incorporate other provisions related to the specific character of joint venture's operations unless these are contrary to Soviet law.

8. The period of operation of a joint venture shall be specified by its partners in an agreement on the establishment thereof or in the joint venture's statute (hereinafter 'foundation documents').

9. As soon as foundation documents come into force, joint ventures established in the territory of the USSR shall be registered with the USSR Ministry of Finance and acquire the rights of a legal entity at the time of registration. Notification on the establishment of joint ventures shall be published in the press.

10. The authorised fund of a joint venture is formed from contributions made by the partners. It can be replenished by using profits derived from business operation of the joint venture and, if necessary, through additional contributions by the partners.

11. The contributions to the authorised fund of a joint venture may include buildings, structures, equipment and other assets, rights to use land, water and other natural resources, buildings, structures and equipment, as well as other proprietary rights (including those to work inventions and use know-how), money assets in the currencies of the partners' countries and in freely convertible currencies.

12. The contribution of a Soviet partner to the authorised fund of a joint venture is evaluated in roubles on the basis of agreed prices with due regard to world market prices. The contribution of the foreign partner is evaluated in the same manner, with the value of the contribution being converted to roubles at the official exchange rate of the USSR State Bank as of the date of signing the agreement to set up the joint venture or as of any other date agreed by the partners. In the absence of information on the current world market prices the value of contributed property is agreed by the partners.

13. Equipment, materials and other property imported into the

USSR by foreign partners in a joint venture as their contribution to the authorised fund of the venture are exempt from custom duties.

14. The property of a joint venture is subject to compulsory insurance with USSR insurance agencies.

15. A joint venture is entitled under Soviet legislation to own, use and dispose of its property in accordance with the objectives of its activities and the purpose of the property. The property of a joint venture shall not be requisitioned or confiscated in an administrative proceeding.

The property rights of a joint venture shall be protected according to Soviet legislative acts protecting state-owned USSR organisations. Execution can be levied on the property of a joint venture only by a decision of bodies empowered under USSR legislation to hear disputes involving joint ventures.

16. Partners in a joint venture shall have the right to assign by common consent, their shares in the joint venture, fully or partially to third parties. In each particular case the assignment of a share is effected with an endorsement of the State Foreign Economic Commission of the USSR Council of Ministers. Soviet partners have the priority right to acquire shares of foreign partners.

If a joint venture is reorganised its rights and obligations shall pass to the legal successors.

17. The industrial property rights, belonging to joint ventures are protected by the Soviet law, including protection in the form of patents. The procedure for the assignment of industrial property rights to a joint venture by partners therein and by a joint venture to partners therein, as well as for commercial working of those rights and their protection abroad is defined by the foundaton documents.

18. A joint venture shall be liable on its obligations in all of its property.

The Soviet State and the partners in a joint venture shall not be liable on its obligations, nor shall a joint venture be liable on the obligations of the Soviet State and of the partners in the venture.

Affiliations of joint ventures established in the territory of the

USSR, which are legal entities, shall not be liable on the obligations of joint ventures, nor shall joint ventures be liable on the obligations of such affiliates.

19. Joint ventures established in the territory of the USSR may set up affiliates and representation offices provided their foundation documents stipulate their right to do so.

Affiliates of joint ventures set up with the participation of Soviet organisations in other countries shall be established in the territory of the USSR in accordance with the rules which apply to the establishment of joint ventures.

20. Disputes between a joint venture and Soviet state-owned, cooperative and other public organisations, disputes among joint ventures, and disputes among partners in a joint venture over matters related to its activities shall be settled according to legislation of the USSR by the USSR courts or, on common consent of both sides, by an arbitration tribunal.

III. Operation of Joint Ventures

21. The governing body of a joint venture is a Board consisting of persons appointed by the partners. Its decision-making procedure is defined by the foundation documents.

The operational activities of a joint venture are governed by a Management consisting of Soviet and foreign citizens.

The Chairman (sic) of the Board and the Director-General shall be citizens of the USSR.

22. A joint venture shall enter into relations with central state authorities of the USSR and of the Union Republics through authorities superior to the Soviet partner in the joint venture. Its contacts with local government authorities and other Soviet organisations shall be direct.

23. A joint venture is independent in developing and approving its business operation programme. State bodies of the USSR shall not fix any mandatory plans of a joint venture nor shall they guarantee the sale of its products.

24. A joint venture is entitled to transact independently in export and import operations necessary for its business activities, including export and import operations in the markets of CMEA member-countries.

The aforementioned export and import operations may also be effected through Soviet foreign trade organisations of the sale network to foreign partners under contractual arrangements.

Shipping into and out of the USSR by a joint venture of goods and other property is effected under licences issued according to legislation of the USSR.

A joint venture is entitled to maintain correspondence, as well as telegraph, teletype and telephone communications with organisations in other countries.

25. All foreign currency expenditures of a joint venture, including transfer of profits and other sums due to foreign partners and specialists, shall be covered by proceeds from sales of the joint venture's products on foreign markets.

26. Sales of products of a joint venture on the Soviet market and supplies to the joint venture from this market of equipment, raw and other materials, components, fuel, energy and other produce shall be effected through respective Soviet foreign trade organisations and paid in roubles on the basis of contractual prices with due regard to world market prices.

27. If necessary, a joint venture may use credits on commercial terms:

in foreign currency – from the USSR Bank for Foreign Trade or, with its consent, from foreign banks and firms:

in roubles – from the USSR State Bank or the USSR Bank for Foreign Trade.

28. The USSR State Bank or the USSR Bank for Foreign Trade shall be authorised to effectuate control as to whether credits extended to a joint venture are used for specified purposes, are secured and repaid in due time.

29. Monetary assets of a joint venture are deposited on its rouble account or currency account with the USSR State Bank and the USSR Bank for Foreign Trade respectively and shall be used for the purposes of the joint venture's operations. The money on the accounts of the joint venture shall bear interest:

in foreign currency – depending on world market rates;

in roubles – on terms and according to the procedure specified by the USSR State Bank.

Fluctuations in exchange rates regarding foreign currency accounts of joint ventures and their operations in foreign currencies shall be carried to their profit and loss accounts.

30. A joint venture shall form a reserve fund and other funds necessary for its operations and for the social development of the collective.

Deductions from profits shall be added to the reserve fund until the latter totals 25 per cent of the authorised fund of the joint venture. The amount of annual deductions to the reserve fund shall be defined by the foundation documents.

The list of other funds and the way they are formed and used shall be specified by the foundation documents.

31. The profits of a joint venture, less the amounts to be attributed to the USSR national budget and sums allocated to form and replenish the joint venture's funds shall be distributed among the partners in proportion to each partner's share in the authorised fund.

32. Foreign partners in a joint venture are guaranteed that amounts due to them as their share in distributed profits of the joint venture are transferable abroad in foreign currency.

33. Joint ventures shall make amortisation deductions under regulations applying to state-owned Soviet organisations, unless a different system is stipulated by the foundation documents. The sums thus accumulated shall remain at the joint venture's disposal.

34. The design and construction of joint venture's facilities, including those intended for social needs, shall be effected through contractual arrangements and paid for with the joint venture's own or loan money. Prior to their approval, designs shall be agreed upon under the procedure established by the USSR State Building Committee. Orders from joint ventures shall receive priority both in regard to limits on construction-assembly work to be carried out by Soviet contruction-assembly organisations and in regard to material resources required for the construction.

35. Cargoes of joint ventures shall be transported under the procedure established for Soviet organisations.

IV. Taxation of Joint Ventures

36. Joint ventures shall pay taxes at the rate of 30 per cent of their profit remaining after deduction to their reserve and other funds intended for the development of production, science and technology. Sums paid in taxes shall be appropriated to the USSR national budget.

Joint ventures shall be exempt from taxes on their profits during the two initial years of their operation.

The USSR Ministry of Finance shall be authorised to reduce the tax rate or to completely exempt from tax individual payers.

37. The assessment of the profit tax shall be effected by a joint venture.

The amounts of the advance tax payment for a current year shall be determined by a joint venture on the basis of its financial plan for a current year.

The assessment of the final tax amount on the profit actually made in an expired calendar year shall be effected by a joint venture not later than March 15 of the year, following the year under review.

38. Financial authorities are empowered to verify tax calculations prepared by joint venture.

Overpaid taxes for the expired year can either be set off against current tax payments, or refunded to the payer at the latter's request.

39. The amount of the profit tax for the current year shall be transferred to the budget by equal instalments not later than 15 days before the end of every quarter. The final amount shall be paid not later than April 1 of the year, following the year under review.

A penalty in the amount of 0.05 per cent for each day of delay shall be recovered for delay of payment.

Collection of the sums of the tax not paid in time shall be carried out conformably (sic) to the procedure prescribed in regard of foreign legal persons by the Rules on Collection of Delayed Taxes and Non-Tax Payments, endorsed by the Decree of the Presidium of the USSR Supreme Soviet of January 26,

1981 (Vedomosti Verkhovnogo Soveta SSSR, 1981, No. 5, Act. 122).

40. A joint venture has the right to appeal against actions of financial authorities in regard to tax collection. An appeal is lodged with the financial authority which verifies the tax calculation. Each case shall be decided within one month from the day the appeal is lodged.

A joint venture is entitled to appeal against the ruling before a superior financial authority within one month from the day of the ruling.

The lodging of an appeal does not suspend the payment of the tax.

41. Unless otherwise provided for by a treaty between the USSR and the respective foreign state, the part of the profit due to a foreign partner in a joint venture, if transferred abroad, shall be taxed at the rate of 20 per cent.

42. The aforementioned taxation procedure shall apply to income made by joint ventures established in the territory of the USSR, and by Soviet-based affiliates of joint ventures set up with the participation of Soviet organisations in other countries as a result of their operations both in the territory of the USSR, on its continential shelf, in the USSR economic zone, and in the territory of other countries.

43. Regulations regarding the taxation of joint ventures shall be issued by the USSR Ministry of Finance.

V. Supervision of Joint Ventures' Operations

44. In order to enable partners in a joint venture to exercise their supervision rights, the foundation documents shall stipulate a procedure for providing partners with information related to the operation of a joint venture, the state of its property, its profits and losses.

A joint venture may set up an audit commission to be formed in a manner defined by the foundation documents.

45. Joint ventures shall keep operational, bookkeeping and statistical records in accordance with the standards established in the

USSR for state-owned Soviet enterprises. The forms of such accounting and bookkeeping shall be jointly specified by the USSR Ministry of Finance and by the USSR Central Board of Statistics.

Joint ventures shall be held responsible under Soviet law for complying with the established accounting and bookkeeping procedure and for the correctness thereof.

Joint ventures shall not submit any accounting or business information to state or other authorities of foreign countries.

46. The auditing of finance, business and commercial activities of joint ventures shall be effectuated (sic) for a fee by the Soviet auditing organisation, operating on a self-supporting basis.

VI. Personnel of Joint Ventures

47. The personnel of joint ventures shall consist mainly of Soviet citizens. The management of a joint venture shall conclude collective agreements with trade union organisations formed at the enterprise. The contents of these agreements, including provisions for the social development of the personnel, are defined by the Soviet legislation and the foundation documents.

48. The pay, routine of work and recreation, social security and social insurance of Soviet employees of joint ventures shall be regulated by Soviet legislation. This legislation shall also apply to foreign citizens employed at joint ventures, except for matters of pay, leave and pensions, which are stipulated by a contract signed with each foreign employee.

The USSR State Committee for Labour and Social Affairs and the All-Union Central Council for Trade Unions shall be authorised to adopt special rules for the application of Soviet social insurance legislation to foreign employees of joint ventures.

49. A joint venture shall make contributions to the USSR national budget for state-sponsored social insurance of Soviet and foreign employees, as well as payments for pensions for Soviet employees in accordance with the rates established for state-owned Soviet organisations. Contributions to cover foreign employees' pensions shall be transferred to respective funds in

the countries of their permanent residence (in these countries' currencies).

50. The pay of foreign employees of a joint venture is subject to income tax at the rate and in accordance with the procedure set up by the Decree of the Presidium of the USSR Supreme Soviet of May 12, 1978 "On the Income Tax Levied on Foreign Legal and Physical Persons" (Vedomosti Verkhovnogo Soveta SSSR, 1978, No. 20, Art. 313). The unspent portion of foreign employees' pay may be transferred abroad in foreign currency.

VII. Liquidation of Joint Ventures

51. A joint venture may be liquidated in cases and in the manner stipulated by the foundation documents, and also by a decision of the USSR Council of Ministers if the activities thereof are not consistent with the objectives defined by these documents. A notification of liquidation of a joint venture shall be published in the press.

52. In the case of liquidation of a joint venture or upon withdrawal from it, the foreign partner shall have the right to the return of his contribution in money or in kind pro rata to the residual balance value of this contribution at the moment of liquidation of the joint venture, after discharging his obligations to the Soviet partners and third parties.

53. The liquidation of a joint venture shall be registered with the USSR Ministry of Finance.

Chairman
of the USSR Council of Ministers N. Ryzhkov

Manager of Operations
of the USSR Council of Ministers M. Smirtiukov

The Kremlin, Moscow, January 13, 1987, No. 49

Appendix 3

Decree (No. 203) of USSR Council of Ministers of 7th March '89 on measures of state control of foreign economic activity
(Unofficial translation)

With the aim of providing effective control over foreign economic activity and the combination of broad economic independence of partners in foreign economic relations with state control of this activity, the USSR Council of Ministers resolves:

1. In accordance with the Decree of the USSR Council of Ministers 2nd December 1988, No. 1405 'On the Further Development of Foreign Economic Activity of State, Cooperative and other Public Enterprises, Unions and Organisations' (SP. USSR – Collection of Decrees, Laws of the USSR, 1989, No. 2 Art. 7), the following system of state control over foreign economic activity is established, including:

Registration of participants in foreign economic relations;
Declarations of goods and other property transferred across the USSR State border;
Rules for export and import of individual types of goods of state importance;
Measures of effective regulation of foreign economic relations.

The stated system is extended to all types of foreign economic activity, including direct production and scientific-technical relations, coastal and cross-border trade, barter operations and to all participants of foreign economic relations (i.e. enterprises, unions, production cooperatives and other organisations directly participating in foreign economic activity, including consortiums, share companies, trading houses, associations of business cooperation with foreign countries, other associations created in the territory of the USSR, joint ventures and international unions and associations).

Registration of Participants in Foreign Economic Relations

2. All those willing to utilise the granted right of independent entry to the foreign market must register with the Ministry of Foreign Economic Relations of the USSR or with their local representative offices.

Registration includes: submission of a registration card, filled out in accordance with the established procedure, receipt of a registration number, inclusion in the officially published state register of participants in foreign economic relationships and issue of a certificate of registration.

The USSR Ministry of Foreign Economic Relations is to:

Have an authorised representative of the Ministry in autonomous regions and areas;
Undertake registration using modern computing equipment and to create a single data bank of registered participants of foreign economic relations.

Registration shall be carried out no later than 30 days from the date of receiving the application. The Ministry of Foreign Economic Relations shall immediately inform the respective area and regional councils, councils of ministers of union and autonomous republics, ministries and organisations of the USSR.

Ministries and organisations, councils of ministers of unions and autonomous republics and local councils must provide all manner of assistance to the USSR Ministry of Foreign Economic Relations and to its local representative offices.

Participants in foreign economic relationships who have received the right to independent entry to the foreign market before the adoption of the present decree shall be registered under the same conditions.

The USSR Minister of Finance, upon registration of joint ventures, international unions and organisations, created in the territory of the USSR, shall also provide for their registration with the USSR Ministry of Foreign Economic Relations as participants in foreign economic relations.

Participants of foreign economic relations are responsible for the authenticity of information presented for registration and upon later changes.

3. To grant the USSR Ministry of Foreign Economic Relations the right to:

Make enquiries, whenever required, of ministries and organisations, councils of ministers of union and autonomous republics, local councils, banks and participants in foreign economic relations, for authenticating information provided in the registration cards;

To levy from the participants in foreign economic relations payments for registration in amounts determined by the USSR Ministry of Foreign Economic Relations in Agreement with the USSR Ministry of Finance, providing compensation for expenses incurred for its completion.

Declaration of Goods and other Property, Transferred across the USSR State Border

4. To establish that from 1 April 1989 goods and other property transferred across the USSR State border are subject to compulsory declaration by way of submission to the offices of the USSR State customs control of a cargo customs declaration of the established format.

Declarations are made by participants in foreign economic relationships independently or on the basis of agreement through all-union foreign economic organisation *Soyuzvneshtrans* of the USSR Ministry of Foreign Economic Relations or by other organisations determined by the offices of the USSR State Customs Control. Goods and other property transferred across the USSR State border without a customs declaration or with violations of the established procedure of declaration are not allowed passage abroad or into the USSR. Entry in the customs declaration of deliberately false statements entails liability under the law. The main directorate of the USSR Customs Control under the USSR Council of Ministers must inform participants in foreign economic relations through the mass media of the rules for making declarations.

5. The offices of the USSR State Customs Control shall take payment for conducting customs procedures, including payments in the currency of the counter agent in volumes determined by the main directorate of the USSR State Customs Control under the USSR Council of Ministers in agreement with the USSR Ministry of Finance.

To permit the main directorate of the State Customs Control under the USSR Council of Ministers to use these means under the established rules with the aim of developing state customs services and the social needs of its employees.

6. To establish that information carried in the cargo customs declaration is the official source data for preparing state statistics of foreign economic activity. The USSR State Committee for Statistics, the USSR Ministry of Foreign Economic Relations, and the main directorate of State Customs Control under the USSR Council of Ministers must provide in 1989–1990 a system of collecting, processing and publication of state statistics of foreign economic activity in a form reflecting modern requirements as to the completeness, authenticity, openness and international comparability of the data.

The Rules for Export and Import of Certain Goods of State Significance

7. To affirm the applied lists of production (works and services), the export and import of which will be conducted in 1989–1990 by enterprises, commercial unions, productions cooperatives and other Soviet organisations on licences granted to them by the appropriate ministries and agencies of the USSR and Councils of Ministers of Union Republics.

To establish that these rules are also applicable to any type of purchase-sale transactions of certain products (works, services) with foreign companies and organisations carried out in Soviet territory.

To permit the State Foreign Economic Commission of the USSR Council of Ministers to introduce certain amendments to the authorised lists of products (works, services).

8. Joint ventures, international commercial unions and organisations created in the territory of the USSR may only export and
import the goods (works, services) they manufacture themselves
and only for their own needs. To conduct intermediary operations a permit of the USSR Ministry of Foreign Economic
Relations is required. Production cooperatives, their unions (con-
glomerates) may export only those products (works, services)
they manufacture themselves. They have no right to purchase
goods with the intent of export, re-sale, nor any right to import
goods for re-sale on the domestic market or conduct intermediary
operations as a type of activity.

Other participants in foreign economic relations must also not
be involved in purchasing goods intended for export, re-sale or
importing state-owned specialised organisations' goods for re-sale
on the USSR domestic market, unless otherwise envisaged in
current regulations.

Measures of effective control of foreign economic relations

9. With the aim of balanced development of foreign economic
relations and perfection of the instruments of implementation of
the state foreign economic policy, immediate measures of control
over foreign economic relationships may be applied in special
cases – the limitation of export/import and suspension of operations of participants in foreign economic relations. Limitations
on export/import may be introduced for certain periods of time
and for certain products (work, services) and for certain states
and groups of states in those cases when required by the payment
relationship or other economic or political conditions and in particular for:

　　controlling demand and supply in the USSR domestic market;
　　effecting international obligations of the USSR connected
　　with control over export or import;
　　achieving mutually beneficial agreements at international
　　trading negotiations;

taking measures against discriminatory acts of foreign states
and (or) their unions.

The above limitations of export/import are effected by the
State Foreign Economic Commission of the USSR Council of
Ministers upon advice from the USSR Ministry of Foreign Economic Relations jointly with the competent state offices in the
form of quantative or price quotas on import or export. All transactions carried out in the framework of filling such quotas are
subject to licensing.

Quotas do not extend to commodities imported into the USSR
in repayment of Soviet credits or to installations under construction on the territory of the USSR.

The articles of the present paragraph do not extend to the
export of produce of joint ventures, international unions and
organisations created on the territory of the USSR, or to the
import of commodities intended for their own use.

10. The State Foreign Economic Commission of the USSR
Council of Ministers on advice of the USSR Ministry of Foreign
Economic Relations, the Council of Ministers of Union may suspend activities of participants in foreign economic relations in
cases of unfair competition or if their activities prejudice the
interests of the state.

Decisions on the discontinuation of activities may be taken in
cases of:

Violation of Soviet legislation on measures of active control
over foreign economic relations of the USSR, non-observance of USSR's international agreements and also the violation of legislation of foreign countries which result in
infringement of economic and political interests of the
USSR;
Conduct of foreign economic activities in violation of the
authorised activities and unsanctioned goods exchange (barter)
operations;
Multiple non-fulfilment of compulsory export supplies with
simultaneous export of similar products in other forms, e.g.
barter instead of cash deal;

Export from the USSR at unjustly low prices and import into the USSR at unjustly high prices;

Multiple export of import of low quality goods;

Provision of deliberately perjurous information in promotional, customs, currency-financial and registrational documentation;

In other cases of violation of Soviet legislation.

Suspension of foreign economic activities may be effected in the form of prohibition of a specific transaction or temporary suspension of all operations of the offender for a period of up to one year. The offender may also be issued a warning without suspension of his foreign economic activity or he may be subject to licensing of export-import operations for a period of up to 6 months. The decision on suspension may be changed or terminated upon showing good cause. Provisions of this paragraph are also applicable to foreign companies and organisations that have committed the said violations in the territory of the USSR.

11. Notification of measures of state control over foreign economic activity are to be available to the public. The USSR Ministry of Foreign Economic Relations and the USSR Chamber of Commerce and Industry must notify Soviet and foreign participants in foreign economic relationships of these measures in good time.

12. The USSR Ministry of Foreign Economic Relations must present for approval of the State Foreign Economic Commission of the USSR Council of Ministers the rules for licensing operations in foreign economic relations through the means of mass media by 20 March 1989.

13. To permit the USSR Ministry of Foreign Economic Relations to purchase in 1989 for the fitting out of the offices of the authorities of the Ministry and its specialised services, filling out the cargo customs declarations, the required equipment and means of communications for the sum of 3.1 million roubles in hard currency on account of general allocations under the currency plan of the Ministry for 1989.

14. The USSR Ministry of Foreign Economic Relations and the USSR Ministry of Justice are to submit within 2 months to the USSR Council of Ministers proposals on changes to the current legislation, required in view of this decree.

Appendix 4

**Decree (No. 1405) of the USSR Council of
Ministers of 2 Dec 1988
(Excerpts)
On the further development of foreign economic
activity of state, cooperative and other public
enterprises, unions and organisations.
(Unofficial translation)**

*Questions on the organisation and activity of joint
ventures, international and union organisations.*

31. With the aim of activating the work on the organisation in the territory of the USSR of joint ventures with the participation of organisations and companies of foreign countries it is determined that:

The shares of Soviet and foreign participants in the authorised capital of the joint venture shall be determined upon agreement between them;

The Chairman of the Board or the Director General of the joint venture may be a foreign citizen;

Principal questions regarding the activity of the joint venture shall be resolved at board meetings on the basis of unanimity of all members of the board;

Questions of employment and dismissal, the forms and sizes of wages and also incentive bonuses in roubles for Soviet employees of the joint ventures shall be decided by the joint venture;

Goods, imported into the USSR by the joint venture for the needs of expanding production may be subject to minimal customs duties or totally exempt;

Payments by foreign employees of joint ventures for accommodation and other services shall be made in roubles, with the exception of cases covered by decisions of the USSR Council of Ministers.

With the aim of additionally stimulating the creation of joint ventures in the far eastern economic region it is deemed necessary to free those ventures from taxation on profits during the first three years from the first declaration of profits.

The Ministry of Finance of the USSR shall:

Draft and approve the rules for determining the taxable income of joint ventures within three months thereof, taking into account the practices of foreign countries;

Decrease by 10 per cent the tax on the profit of joint ventures created in the far eastern region.

32. It is deemed necessary to give the USSR Ministry of Finance the right not to tax for a certain period of time that part of the profit destined for the foreign partner of the joint venture at the point of its transfer abroad or to lower the size of the said taxation if not otherwise stated in agreements between the USSR and the respective state. This right to be mostly applied to joint venture production of consumer goods, medical equipment, pharmaceuticals, hi-tech products having important domestic economic applications and also to joint ventures located in the far eastern economic region.

33. To establish that the transfer of the shares of a joint venture, the insurance against risks in a joint venture and also the auditing of financial and economic activity are undertaken upon agreement of the sides.

34. The main directorate of the state customs control under the USSR Council of Ministers in conjunction with the Ministry of Finance of the USSR is to provide customs privileges to the foreign personnel of joint ventures.

35. To give the right to state enterprises, unions and organisations to reach decisions on the creation of joint ventures, international unions and organisations with foreign organisations and companies upon agreement of the senior controlling body.

Manufacturing cooperatives may create joint ventures, international unions and organisations with the participation of foreign organisations and companies with the respective consent of the council of ministers of the union republic without regional divisions, the council of ministers of the autonomous republic, the area or regional council, Moscow or Leningrad city council, all in accordance with the location of the cooperative, or with the agreement of the Minstry, the enterprise (organisation, office) under the auspices of which the cooperative has been registered.

Appendix 5

The rules of crediting and payment of joint ventures, international unions and organisations of USSR and other countries – Comecon members, and also joint ventures with the participation of Soviet organisations and companies of western and developing countries (Excerpts) (Unofficial translation)

The present rules regulate the organisation of payment and crediting in roubles and in hard currency for joint ventures in the course of production and sales of the products and also the financing and crediting of capital investments.

Chapter 1 – Short-term Rouble Loans

1.2 The crediting of joint ventures is effected by banks at the location of the bank accounts of the joint ventures.

The bank pays an annual 0.5 per cent interest on the current accounts of joint ventures.

1.3 Short-term credits to joint ventures in roubles are given for the purposes of payment for covering and against surplus raw materials, uncompleted production, future expenditure, other reserves and expenditure on production, for goods shipped inside the country, the period for the repayment of which had not yet arrived, for opening letters of credit.

1.8 The checking on the provision of credits is conducted in accordance with Appendix No.4 on a monthly basis from the balance of the venture and information (Appendix No.3) presented simultaneously with the balance.

1.12 Joint ventures failing to discharge overdue debts on bank credits for over 2 months are not issued with new credits. The incoming revenue goes towards covering the overdue debts on the credits.

1.14 The crediting of export operations is undertaken on a separate credit account with no limits.

1.15 To provide for the payment of goods sold abroad on condition of payment in instalments, the joint venture must receive guarantees of foreign banks.

Chapter 2 – Financing Capital Investments

2.4 Credits for joint ventures in roubles are provided by the bank:

for the construction of production facilities for a period of 6 years from the date of issuing the first credit;
for the development of the material-technical basis of the social sphere in the amount of up to 75 per cent of the construction cost for a period of up to 6 years from the date of completion of repayment of credits from the general income of the joint ventures.

2.6 The mangement of the bank may approve delays in repayment of debts within the overall period of time the credit is issued for.

Chapter 3 – Hard Currency Loans

3.1 A joint venture may use credits in hard currency received by them on commercial conditions from USSR *Vnesheconombank* or, with its consent, from foreign banks and firms. The source for covering the credits is the revenue from the sale of export products.

3.2 Short-term credits in hard currency for the purchase abroad of raw materials and other goods are issued by *Vnesheconombank* for a period of up to 2 years.

3.3 Joint ventures may be issued with medium-term and long-term credits for the payment of imported equipment, machines, licences and other goods, and also services, required for improving and expanding production.

3.4 In the case of a joint venture having uncovered debt the USSR *Vnesheconombank* had the right to use, for covering this debt, any hard currency funds available on the account of the joint venture with USSR *Vnesheconombank*.

3.6 Upon issuing a credit in hard currency the USSR *Vnesheconombank* draws from the joint venture a facility fee for the undertaking in the amount of 0.5 per cent p.a. of the unused portion of the credit.

3.13 In the absence of hard currency funds on the account of the joint venture, the amount not covered in due time is carried to the account of the hard currency debt with additional annual interest of 3 per cent over the established percentage fixed in the credit agreement. The bank also has the right not to grant further credit and to credit all revenues towards payment of the existing debt.

Chapter 4

4.3 Interest is paid on hard currency accounts at levels established by the USSR *Vnesheconombank*.

Appendix 6

USSR law on property

This law was passed on the 6th March 1990 and came into force on the 1st July 1990. The following is an unofficial translation of parts of the law.

Chapter 1 General Provisions

Art.1 The right of property
1. The right of property in the USSR is recognised and protected by law.
2. The property owner at his choice owns, uses and disposes of the property which belongs to him.

   The property owner has the right to conduct any activity in relation to his property which does not contradict the law. He may use property to conduct economic or other activity not forbidden by law.
3. In certain cases, upon the conditions and within the limits envisaged by law, the property owner may be put under obligation to permit limited usage of his property by other persons.
4. The property owner has the right on conditions and within limits envisaged by legislative acts of the USSR, union and autonomous republics to make agreements with citizens on using their labour in the course of the exercise of the right of property which belongs to him.

   Irrespective of the form of property on the basis of which the labour of a citizen is used, he is provided with payment and conditions of labour and also other socio-economic guarantees, envisaged by the current legislation.
5. The implementation of the right of property should not damage the environment, violate the laws and the interests of citizens, enterprises, institutions, organisations and the state, as protected by law.

6.The usage of any form of property must exclude the estrangement of a worker from the means of production and of exploitation of a person by a person.

Art. 2 Legislation of the USSR, Union and Autonomous Republics on property

1. By the present law, in accordance with the USSR constitution, the main principles of property in force in the whole territory of the USSR are established.
2. The relationships of property not covered by the present law are regulated by the published legislative acts of the USSR, union and autonomous republics, in accordance with this law.
3. The particulars of enacting property rights for historical and cultural monuments are established by special legislation of the USSR, union and autonomous republics.
4. Relationships concerning the creation and usage of inventions, discoveries, works of science, literature, art and other subjects of intellectual property are regulated by the special legislation of the USSR, union and autonomous republics.

Art. 3. Objects of the right of property

1. Ownership may be of land, its resources, water, flora, and fauna, buildings, structures, equipment, objects of material and spiritual culture, money, securities, and other property.
2. The results of economic usage of property (production and profits) if not otherwise envisaged by law or agreement, belong to the owner of this property.

Art. 4. The subjects of the law on property. Types of ownership

1. Property in the USSR is represented in the form of the ownership by Soviet citizens, collective and state property.
   In the USSR there may be ownership of property by foreign states, international organisations, foreign legal entities and citizens.
2. Uniting of property which is owned by citizens, legal entities and the state is permitted, as is the creation on this basis of mixed forms of ownership, including the ownership of joint ventures

with the participation of Soviet legal entities and foreign legal entities and citizens.

3. Legislative acts of union and autonomous republics may establish other forms of property, not envisaged by the present law.

4. Property may be owned on the basis of communal (share or joint) property by several persons simultaneously, irrespective of the type of property.

5. The state creates conditions, necessary for the development of various forms of ownership and provides for their protection.

Art. 5. Proceedings against the property of an owner

1. To enforce the obligations of a legal entity proceedings may be taken against any property belonging to it whether on the rights of property or full economic management and also effective control other than in the case as stated in Art 26. of the present law.

The owner is not responsible for the undertakings of legal entities created by him and they are not responsible for undertakings of the property owner, with exception of cases envisaged by legislative acts of the USSR, union and autonomous republics.

2. Citizens are responsible for their undertakings with the property belonging to them on the right of property.

The list of property of citizens, upon which proceedings may not be directed following demands of creditors, is established by legislative acts of union and autonomous republics.

Chapter 2. Property of citizens of the USSR

Art. 7.

Property of citizens may consist of residential houses, garden houses, *dachas* (country houses), plantations on the land plots, transportation means, money, shares, other securities, objects of home use and personal use, production means for peasant and labour farming, personal farming, individual and other economic activity and also the finished products and receipts and other production property of consumer or other use.

Art. 8. Property of a labour economy

A labour economy is conducted by members of a family and other persons who conduct business jointly. They may own:

A workshop, other small enterprise in the area of social service, trade, public food outlets and other areas of economic activity, residential buildings and economic structures, means of transportation, raw materials, materials and other property.

Section 3. Collective property

The subject of collective property may be a lease enterprise, a collective enterprise, a cooperative, a stock company, an economic society or enterprise, social organisations and other unions which are legal entities.

Chapter 5. Property of joint ventures, foreign citizens, organisations and states

Art. 27. Property of joint ventures

Joint ventures with the participation of Soviet legal entities and foreign legal entities and citizens are created in the territory of the USSR in the form of joint-stock companies, economic societies and associations and may have as property that property which is required for conducting the activity set out in the statutory documents.

Art. 28. Property of foreign citizens

The principles of the present law relevant to the property of Soviet citizens are also applied to the property of foreign citizens which is located in the USSR. The principles of peasant and other industrial economy is applied to the property of foreign citizens permanently resident in the USSR.

Art. 29. Property of foreign legal entities

Foreign legal entities have the right to have as property in the territory of the USSR industrial and other enterprises, buildings, structures and other property for the purposes of conducting by means of them economic and other activity in the cases and under the rules established by legislative acts of the USSR.

Art. 30. *Property of foreign states and international organisations*

Foreign states and international organisations have the right to own on the territory of the USSR as property, that property which is necessary for conducting diplomatic, consular and other international relationships in the cases and order as established by international agreements and legislative acts of the USSR and union republics.

Chapter 6. *Guarantees of protection of property rights*

Art. 31. *The guarantee of property rights*

1. The state guarantees the stability of property rights established in accordance with the present law.

2. In the case of enacting by the USSR, union or autonomous republic of laws terminating the property rights, the damages incurred by the property owner as a result of the adoption of such acts, upon a court decision, will be remitted to the owner in full by the USSR, the respective union or autonomous republic.

3. The state provides equal protection of the property right in the legislation to citizens, organisations and other property holders.

Art. 32. *Protection of property right.*

1. The property owner has the right to demand his property from an alien and unlawful possessor in accordance with the civil legislation of the USSR, union and autonomous republics.

2. The property holder may demand the removal of any violations of his right, even when these violations may not be connected with the loss of his property.

3. The protection of property right is effected in court, by state arbitration or by a tertiary court.

4. The rights, envisaged by the present article, belong also to the person, who may not be the property owner, but owning property on the right of full economic management, operative control, life-long inheritable ownership or on another basis, envisaged by law or agreement. This person also has the right to protection of his property against the property owner.

Appendix 7

USSR law on land

This law was passed on 28 February 1990 and came into force on 15 March 1990. The following is an unofficial translation of part of the law.

Chapter 1. General provisions

Article 1. Land legislation of the USSR, union and autonomous republics

Land relationships in the USSR are regulated by the present basis and other legislation of USSR, union and autonomous republics, published in accordance with this basis.

Article 2. The structure of land of the USSR.

In accordance with special purposes all lands in the USSR are divided into:

1 Land of agricultural application;
2 Land of residential areas (towns, town-type settlements, and rural settlements);
3 Land of industry, transportation, communications, defence and other purposes;
4 Land of nature reserves, health and recreational purposes and of historical-cultural significance;
5 Land of forest reserve;
6 Areas of water reserve;
7 Land in reserve.

In places of residence and enterprise activity of minority peoples and ethnic groups the legislation of union and autonomous republics may establish special conditions of usage of the said categories of land.

Article 3. Land is the property of the people

Land is the property of the people living on the particular territory.

Every citizen of the USSR has the right to a plot of land, the conditions and rules for provision of which are determined by the present basis and the legislation of union and autonomous republics.

Article 4. The legal right of councils of people's deputies in disposing of land

Councils of People's Deputies provide land plots for ownership and usage to citizens of the USSR, collective farms, state farms and other state, cooperative and public enterprises, institutions and organisations, and, in cases established by legislation – to other organisations and persons.

Councils of People's Deputies withdraw land plots in accordance with the present basis, legislation of union and autonomous republics.

The provision and withdrawal of land at places of residence and economic activity of minority peoples and ethnic groups for purposes not connected with their main area of activity, can be undertaken as a result of a referendum amongst such peoples and ethnic groups with the consent of the respective councils of people's deputies.

Article 5. Ownership of land

Lifetime inheritable ownership of land is provided to citizens of the USSR for aims set out in Article 20 of the present basis.

Maximum sizes of land plots to be provided are determined by the legislation of union and autonomous republics.

Permanent ownership of land is given to collective farms, state farms, to other state, cooperative and public enterprises, institutions and organisations, to religious organisations to conduct agriculture and forestry.

Article 6. Usage of land

Permanent or temporary usage of land is provided to:

Citizens of the USSR for purposes described in Articles 21 and 22 of the present basis;

Industrial, transportational and other non-agricultural reasons, cooperative and public enterprises, institutions and organisations;

For the needs of defence for organisations listed in Article 31 of the present basis;

Religious organisations;

Joint ventures, international unions and organisations with the participation of Soviet and foreign legal entities.

Article 7. Leasing of land

Land for temporary usage on conditions of lease is provided to citizens of the USSR, collective and state farms and other state, cooperative and public enterprises, institutions and organisations, joint ventures, international unions and organisations with the participation of Soviet and foreign legal entities and also to foreign states, international organisations, foreign legal entities and citizens.

The lessors of the land are the respective councils of people's deputies.

Conditions of lease are determined by agreement of the sides and are secured in an agreement. The lease holder has the priority right of extending the agreement of lease on the land upon expiration of the agreement.

Leased land plots for agricultural purposes upon agreement of the sides may be transferred into ownership of the lease holder.

Collective and state farms and other state and cooperative agricultural enterprises may secure land with certain workers and leasing groups as an internal division of land.

Relationships on land leasing are regulated by the present basis, the basis of legislation of the USSR, union republics on leasing and by the legislation of union and autonomous republics.

Article 8. Provision of lands.

The provision of land plots for ownership and usage is undertaken by way of allotment.

The provision of a land plot, being under ownership or lease to another land owner or land user is undertaken only following the withdrawal of this plot under the rules established in Articles 11 and 24 of the present basis.

Lands fit for agricultural usage must be provided for agricultural needs in the first instance.

The right of ownership and the right of permanent usage of land is confirmed by a state deed.

The form of the state deed, the rules for its registration and issue are determined by the legislation of union republics. The form and rules for registration of agreements for the leasing of land and other temporary usage of land are determined by the legislation of union and autonomous republics.

Article 9. Termination of the right of ownership and the right of land usage

The right of ownership and the right of usage of the complete land plot or part of it is terminated by the council of people's deputies in the cases of:

1 Voluntary relinquishment of the land plot.
2 Expiration of the period of time for which the land plot was given.
3 Termination of activity of the enterprise, institution, organisation or peasant farm.
4 Use of land contrary to the purpose it was provided for.
5 Termination of working relationships subject to which the working plot was provided, unless otherwise determined by the legislation of the USSR, union or autonomous republic.
6 Irrational use of the land, manifesting itself in the case of agricultural use in lower than normal harvest levels (in accordance with the official evaluation).
7 Use of the land in ways that decrease the fertility of the soil, or cause its chemical or radioactive contamination, and worsening of the ecological situation.
8 Systematic failure to pay land tax at the times set out by legislation of union and autonomous republics and also of lease payments in the time-scale established in the lease agreement.

9 Non-use for one year of land provided for agricultural production and for two years for non-agricultural production.
10 Withdrawal of lands in cases envisaged in the present basis.

Points 6 and 9 of this article do not extend to the right of ownership of land by citizens, maintaining a peasant farm during 3 years from receiving the land.

The right to use of leased land also terminates upon cancellation of a lease agreement in cases envisaged in the legislation of the USSR and union republics on leasing.

The legislation of union and autonomous republics may envisage other cases of termination of the right of ownership, the right of usage and lease of land.

Article 10. Transfer of the right of ownership and right of use of land

Upon transfer of the right of ownership of a building or structure, together with these objects the right of ownership or use of the land is transferred under the rules and on conditions set out in the legislation of union and autonomous republics.

Article 11. Withdrawal of land

The withdrawal of land for state and public needs is undertaken upon decision of the respective council of people's deputies with the consent of the landowner or upon agreement of the land user under the rules established by the legislation of the USSR, union and autonomous republics.

The withdrawal of agricultural lands for non-agricultural needs may be allowed only in extreme circumstances in accordance with the legislation of the union and autonomous republics.

A landowner or/and user aggrieved by the decision of the council of peoples' deputies may appeal to the court.

The withdrawal of highly productive land, determined in accordance with the official evaluation level for that area, and also of land occupied by specially protected natural or historic-cultural objects is not permitted. A list of such land is established by the legislation of union and autonomous republics.

The withdrawal of suburban and green-belt areas, research

fields of scientific research establishment and teaching institutions, forests of the first category for state and public needs are permitted only in exceptional circumstances under the rules established by the legislation of union and autonomous republics.

Enterprises, institutions and organisations, interested in the withdrawal of land must, prior to commencement of planning, receive preliminary consent of the landowners and the land users and also from the local councils of people's deputies to the location of the structure, the approximate size of the plot and the conditions of its allotment, taking into account the complex development of the territory. The financing of planning works before the preliminary agreement is not permitted.

The withdrawal of lands from collective and state farms and other agricultural enterprises in order to make them available to Soviet citizens and agricultural cooperatives is undertaken by the regional or town council of people's deputies in the cases and under the rules established by the present basis and the legislation of union and autonomous republics.

Article 12. Land tax and rental payments

Ownership and use of land in the USSR require payment. Payment for land is levied in the form of land tax or lease tax, dependent on the quality and location of the land.

The imposition and amount of tax are set by the legislation of the union and autonomous republics. The lessee pays rent, the amount of which is determined on agreement of the sides and within limits established by the legislation of union and autonomous republics.

Payment for forest reserve land is levied as part payment for using the forests.

Payments for land are paid into the budgets of local councils of people's deputies and may be partially centralised in the budgets of union and autonomous republics and are directed in the first instance towards the protection of land, the improvement of its quality, the material encouragment of landowners and land users, including the lessees, for undertaking such actions and also towards land tenure and the social development of the area.

The legislation of union and autonomous republics may envisage privileges in levying payment for land; partial or complete liberation for a fixed period, delays in payment, lowering of the land tax rate.

Payment is not due from nature reserves, national parks, botanical gardens and also enterprises, institutions and organisations, groups and citizens who have received ownership or lease of damaged or low productive land. Under the rules established by the legislation of union and autonomous republics, upon decision of council of people's deputies, payment may be exempted for closed nature reserves, experimental enterprises of scientific research establishments and teaching institutions of agricultural nature, cultural and educational and health care establishments and also enterprises dealing in traditional crafts at places of residence and enterprise of minority peoples and ethnic groups, other enterprises, institutions and organisations and citizens of the USSR.

[The following are just excerpts and summaries]

Article 13. Local councils and their responsibilities
Must provide land to citizens and legal entities (organisations), undertake registration, receive payments for the lands, control the use and (as above) withdraw land.

Article 14. Union and autonomous republic councils
Are in charge of land within their borders (internal divisions, monitoring soil conditions, state registry, USSR legislation, universal land prices throughout USSR).

Chapter 2. The rights and obligations of landowners and land users

Article 16. Rights and obligations of landowners
A landowner has the right of ownership to produce products and the revenue from their sale; has the right to lease his land for temporary use to other parties; right to build structures on this land – both residential and industrial.

Article 18. Protection of rights of landowners
Interference from other control bodies is forbidden except when the law is violated.

Article 19. Guarantee of ownership
Withdrawal of land from citizens may be conducted only upon provision of an equivalent plot with equivalent structures on it (ie. full compensation for loss) – same for legal entities.

Chapter 3. Land ownership and usage by USSR citizens

Article 20. Land ownership by USSR citizens
USSR Citizens have the right to life-long ownership of land for:

- peasant farms (for sale also);
- personal agricultural use;
- for building and maintenance of a residential house;
- for gardening and keeping of livestock;
- for a dacha (country house);
- in cases of receipt as inheritance or purchase of a house;
- for traditional occupations (handicraft typical for that particular area, basket weaving, etc. indigenous to that place).

Article 21. Land usage
Citizens may receive land plots for agricultural and other needs.

Chapter 4. Land for agricultural use

Article 23. Provision of agricultural lands
To:
USSR Citizens;
Cooperatives;
State and collective farms;
(joint ventures are legal entities, but no specific mention is made);
for purposes directly related to agriculture.

Article 25. Land ownership by citizens maintaining a peasant farm
Plots provided to them are not subject to partition.

Article 26. Rules for Provison of land for peasant farming
Land is provided on the basis of an application to the local council. Refusal to provide land may be taken to court.

Chapter 8. Forest reserves, water reserves and reserve land

Article 36. Lands of forest reserves
Local councils may provide forest reserves for temporary usage for agricultural usage.

Section 15. International agreements

Article 54. International agreements
International agreements have primacy over the present law. If the international agreement of a union republic with another state establishes rules other than those in the republican land legislation, then the international agreement is applied.

Appendix 8

Draft joint venture agreement

The following is a sample form of a joint venture agreement between Soviet and Western partners.

Although this text does cover the points that are usually included in such an agreement and could serve as a basis for negotiations, no transaction of the type envisaged (anywhere in general and in the USSR in particular) should be embarked upon without first seeking proper professional advice.

Agreement

On the establishment of joint venture 'Inter-Acme Plastic'

1. Parties
1.1 THE COOPERATIVE 'MOSKOVSKY' of Moscow USSR a legal entity duly registered in the City of Moscow USSR in accordance with the Law on Cooperation (hereinafter called 'X');
1.2 XYZ plc of London, England a public limited company duly incorporated under the laws of England (hereinafter called 'Y').

2. Recitals
The parties to this Agreement have agreed to establish a joint venture, to be located at_____in the City of Moscow, under the laws of the Soviet Union to be known, in English, as 'INTER-ACME PLASTIC' and, in Russian, as_____subject to the terms and conditions hereinafter set out.

3. Definitions
In this Agreement the following expressions shall have the following meanings:

3.1 'Agreement' – this Agreement including the Recitals and Appendices.

3.2 'Appendix(ces)' – an Appendix or the Appendices to this Agreement and forming an integral hereof.

3.3 'Feasibility Study' – the Feasibility Study (Appendix 'A') which has been formulated by the Parties.

3.4 'Internal and External Markets' – the USSR and world markets.

3.5 'J.V.' – the joint venture 'INTER-ACME PLASTIC' to be established by the Parties in accordance with this Agreement.

3.6 'J.V. Documents' shall comprise this Agreement, the Statutes and any other documents which the Parties shall in writing agree shall be deemed to be incorporated within the J.V. documents.

3.7 'The Joint Venture Law' shall mean the decrees and resolution referred to in Clause 6.1 below including any subsequent amendments thereto and any other relevant normative laws.

3.8 'Parties'– X and Y.

3.9 'The Products' shall be deemed to include all products, merchandise, goods, wares, commodities and services manufactured, produced, rendered or in any manner undertaken by the J.V. as described in Appendix 'B' and additions that may be made thereto in the future.

3.10 'Statutes' – the Statutes (Appendix 'C') drawn up by the Parties and which establish the internal rules and regulations of the management administration and operation of the J.V.

4. Declaration of the Parties

The Parties hereby declare that will establish the J.V. in the City of Moscow, USSR and that the J.V. will accord with the laws of the Soviet Union as from the time of its registration.

5. The aims and objectives of the J.V.

5.1 The aims and objectives of business and activity, of the J.V. shall be to establish a production base plant and facility for the production of the Products and to establish a distribution and marketing service for the Products in the Internal and External Markets for the sale of the Products and to develop and achieve maximum sales of the Products for the benefit of the J.V.

5.2 The Parties agree that they shall use their best endeavours to promote in all respects both in the Internal and External Markets the sale of the Products in order to achieve maximum possible sales in Soviet currency and particularly in freely convertible currencies in order to meet the remittance of Y's share in the profits of the J.V. to Y in such type of currency.

6. The legal status of the J.V.

6.1 The J.V. shall be established as a legal entity pursuant to this Agreement and to the laws of the Soviet Union and in particular;

6.1.1 The Decree of the Presidium of the USSR Supreme Soviet dated the 13th day of January 1987 'On Questions Concerning the Establishment in the Territory of the USSR and Operation of Joint Ventures, International Amalgamations and Organisations with the participation of Soviet and Foreign Organisations Firms and Management Bodies'.

6.1.2 The Decree of the USSR Council of Ministers dated 13th day of January 1987 number 49 'On the Establishment in the Territory of the USSR and Operation of Joint Ventures with the Participation of Soviet Organisations and Firms from Capitalist and Developing Countries' as amended.

6.1.3 The Resolution of the CPSU Central Committee and the Council of Ministers of the Soviet Union dated the 17th day of September 1987 number 1074 'On Additional Measures to Improve Foreign Activities under the New Conditions of the Management of the Country's Economy' and Decree No. 203 of the USSR Council of Ministers dated 7th March 1989 'On Measures of Control of Foreign Economic Activities'.

6.2 The J.V. may in its own name purchase take on lease or in exchange hire or otherwise acquire and hold any interest right privilege concession patent right licence secret process machinery plant stock in trade and any real or personal property of any kind necessary or convenient for the purpose of and in connection with the business of the J.V. and shall be entitled in its own name to sue and be sued in any court of competent jurisdiction and within the jurisdiction of the arbitrator pursuant to the terms of arbitration established in the Agreement.

6.3 In the event that the law of the Soviet Union is silent on any matter which may relate to affect or be concerned in the establishment undertaking operation and liquidation of the J.V. the Parties hereto shall be subject to such terms and conditions as shall be enacted in the Statutes and the terms and conditions of this Agreement. In the event that there shall be any conflict between the terms and conditions of the J.V. documents and the laws of the Soviet Union then it is hereby agreed and declared that the laws of the Soviet Union shall prevail AND IT IS FURTHER HEREBY AGREED AND DECLARED that in the event that any matter shall arise upon which the laws of the Soviet Union shall remain silent and which are not dealt with under the terms and conditions of the J.V. documents then the Parties hereto shall use their best endeavours to resolve the matter by agreement in writing and in default thereof such matter or matters shall be referred to the arbitrator who shall in his sole discretion determine such matter or matters in accordance with the terms of arbitration hereinafter appearing.

6.4 The liability of the J.V. shall be determined as follows:

6.4.1 The J.V. shall be responsible and liable upon all obligations entered into undertaken or for which it may be liable under the laws of the Soviet Union.

6.4.2 The Soviet Union (and the Parties) shall not be liable in respect of any matters or obligations of the J.V.

6.4.3 The J.V. shall not be responsible or liable for any responsibilities or obligations of the Soviet Union (and of the Parties).

6.5 The J.V. shall have its trade emblem a logo in the form appearing in Appendix 'D'.

6.6. The J.V. shall be entitled to pursue and undertake its purposes as hereinbefore defined upon the premise that it shall be responsible for its capitalisation and self financing in accordance with its aims and objectives.

6.7 The annual budget of the J.V. shall be prepared in accordance with its aims and objectives and shall be determined in writing not less than one calendar month before the commencement of each financial year of the J.V. such budget incorporating current income and expenditure in roubles and foreign currency.

6.8 The J.V. shall at the commencement of each calendar year prepare and agree a production programme which programme shall be determined by reference to previous sales and sales forecast to be provided by the Parties.

6.9 In the event that there shall be any conflict between the terms and conditions of this Agreement and the Statutes then the Parties hereto agree and declare that the provisions of this Agreement shall prevail in such circumstances.

7. Distributors Agents and representative offices

7.1 The J.V. may appoint distributors and agent traders for the purpose of maximising sales and marketing of the Products in the Internal and External Markets but any such appointment shall operate and be undertaken in accordance with all rules and regulations contained in the J.V. documents and in the event that the J.V. shall open undertake and manage a branch office or other place of business within the Soviet Union such branch office or place of business shall be the object of all requisite approvals of any local authority of competent jurisdiction within the Soviet Union.

7.2 The Parties hereto agree that any such appointment pursuant to subclause 7.1 above shall clearly state the legal status of the appointee and further any such appointment shall clearly state that the appointee will not be responsible or liable in any manner upon the obligations of the J.V. and neither shall the J.V. be responsible or liable upon the obligations of the appointee.

7.3 In the event that the Parties hereto shall determine by agreement to operate and undertake a branch office or other place of business such business shall be undertaken in the sole name of the J.V. and in no other behalf.

8. The authorised fund

8.1 In order to establish the financial standing and capitalisation of the J.V. and its business undertaking the J.V. shall be capitalised and be established as follows:

The Authorised Fund of the J.V. shall be capitalised in the sum of _____ roubles and the title and property in the capitalised sums shall become vested in and become the property of the J.V.

8.2 The shares of the Parties hereto in the Authorised Fund shall be as follows:

    8.2.1 X   −%

    8.2.2 Y   −%

8.3 The contributions of the Parties hereto to the Authorised Fund shall be made up as follows:

    8.3.1 X shall contribute   roubles in cash and (here specify any buildings land leases machinery equipment and other resources) which for the purposes of calculating X's share in the Authorised Fund are valued at   roubles

    8.3.2 Y shall contribute £   (which for the purposes of calculating Y's share in the Authorised Fund shall be deemed to have been converted to roubles at the official exchange rate of the pound sterling against the rouble as determined by the State Bank of the Soviet Union.) That exchange rate is presently £1 = R1 but if the said official exchange rate shall be different at the time the said amount is paid into the J.V.'s bank account the shares of the Parties in the Authorised Fund as referred to in Clause **8.2.** above shall accordingly be proportionally adjusted and (here specify any equipment stocks production machinery patents trade marks knowhow and any other resources) which for the purpose of calculating Y's share in the Authorised Fund are valued at   roubles.

8.4 The capital sums hereinbefore referred to in sub-clauses 8.3.1 and 8.3.2 shall be remitted to the bankers to the J.V. being *Vnesheconombank* of the Soviet Union within 28 days from the date of registration of the J.V. with the Ministry of Finance of the Soviet Union.

8.5 In the event that J.V. shall require further injection of capital monies the Parties hereto agree that X shall be required to contribute no more than   % and Y shall be required to contribute no more than   % by way of contribution to such further injections of capital monies PROVIDED THAT such percentages may be altered having regard for any exchange rate differential as referred to in Clause 8.3.2. above.

8.6 Any assets equipment or other materials which shall be provided by the Parties hereto in accordance with the terms of subclause 8.3 hereof shall be brought into account in the books of the J.V. at the values referred to in clauses 8.3.1 and 8.3.2. above which have been agreed between the Parties hereto with due regard to current world market prices and valuations.

9. Determination and distribution of profits and losses and establishment of funds

9.1 Pursuant to the decree of the Council of Ministers of the Soviet Union dated the 13th day of January 1987 being numbered 49 referred to in Clause 6.1.2 above all monies for the benefit of the J.V. shall be derived from Authorised Fund referred to in Clause 5 hereof and from profits achieved by the J.V. and all distributions from any such profits shall be determined by a decision of the Parties by reference to the annual accounts of the J.V.

9.2 The Parties hereby agree as follows:

9.2.1 The J.V. shall establish a reserve fund in each financial year and which shall not exceed 25% of the Authorised Fund referred to in Clause 8 hereof. Such fund shall be available to meet any losses of the J.V. and any items of unexpected expenditure.

9.2.2 The J.V. shall establish a production development fund which shall serve as a fund for the purchase of new plant and machinery for the improved manufacture of the products and to make provision for interest payments on any loans secured by the J.V. for the purchase of plant and equipment but the production development fund shall not in any one year exceed   - % of the profits disclosed in the accounts of the J.V.

9.2.3 The J.V. shall establish a material incentives fund which shall be utilised to pay annual bonuses to any employees of the J.V. who achieve agreed production levels and further to provide a reserve fund for aid and assistance to employees of the J.V. who may encounter financial difficulties such as the J.V. shall merit affording assistance unto and the amount to be allocated to such material incentives fund shall be determined on an annual basis.

9.2.4 The J.V. shall establish a social and cultural development fund to be utilised to assist and develop in social amenities for the employees of the J.V. and the amount to be allocated to such social and cultural development fund shall be determined on an annual basis.

9.3 The Board of the J.V. as hereinafter determined may by unanimous decision determine at the end of each financial year of the J.V. any other distribution of profits to any other reserve fund but in making any such decision the Board shall first consider the requirements of the J.V. to reinvest any profits for the growth and advancement of the business of the J.V.

9.4 The J.V. shall pay all the lawful taxes due under the laws of the Soviet Union on any profits disclosed in the annual accounts of the J.V. after first deducting distributions to the reserve fund hereinbefore described and any other funds, the establishment of which does not contravene the laws of the Soviet Union, which are created by the J.V. for the development of production and scientific and technological research in respect of the products. The J.V. shall be exempt from paying any taxes on profits of the J.V. for two years from the first year in which it makes a profit.

9.5 Any profits remaining after deduction of Soviet taxes shall be apportioned between the Parties hereto in accordance with their percentage contributions to the Authorised Fund referred to Clause 8 hereof.

9.6 The Parties agree that 28 days after the auditors to the J.V. certify the accounts of the J.V. for the financial year in question and there results a profit after deduction of the reserve and other funds the auditors for the time being of the J.V. shall certify the apportionment of the profit between the Parties. In the event that such profit is not available in non-Soviet currency such share shall be transferred in roubles to the account of Y with *Vnescheconombank* of the Soviet Union or Y may be compensated in such other manner as the Parties shall lawfully agree.

9.7 In the event that the annual accounts of the J.V. shall disclose losses then the Parties agree that such losses shall be met out of the reserve fund but that if such reserve fund is insufficient to cover the said loss the Parties hereto shall use their best endeavours to meet such losses out of trading income or out of the capital monies standing to the credit of the J.V.

10. Management and board

10.1 The administration, government, direction and management of the J.V. shall be undertaken by the Board of the J.V. ('the Board') and the management commission ('the Management') and the appointment and duties of the Board and the Management shall be determined as follows:

10.2 The government and decisions of the J.V. shall be undertaken by the Board which shall be composed of _____ Directors to be nominated from time to time by X and _____ Directors to be nominated from time to time by Y.

10.3 Within the period of ____ days after registration of the J.V. with the USSR Ministry of Finance X and Y shall each notify the other the names of the Directors to be nominated by them.

10.4 The Board shall be responsible within ____ days of the registration of the J.V. to appoint and elect one of its members as Chair of the Board and one other member as Deputy Chair and the Parties hereto agree that the post of Chair may be filled from the Directors representing in the first case Y or in the second case X and the post of Deputy Chairman may be filled from the Directors representing in the first case X and in the second case Y. It is further agreed and declared that the appointment of Chair and Deputy Chair may be changed from time to time by agreement of the Board.

10.5 The powers rights and duties of the Board are specified in the Statutes.

10.6 The powers rights and duties of the Chair and Deputy Chair are specified in the Statutes.

10.7 The members of the Board shall be entitled to receive:

10.7.1 remuneration at the rates and upon the terms to be agreed from time to time between the Parties hereto;

10.7.2 bonus payments to be paid annually and by reference to the performance of the J.V. and any profits achieved by the J.V. in its previous financial year as disclosed in the annual accounts of the J.V.

10.8 The responsibility of the management shall be undertaken by a Director General who shall be appointed by the Board and who shall be responsible for the day to day management of the

J.V. in accordance with the Statutes and the policies and principles laid down by the Board.

10.9 The day to day activities of the personnel and employees and any regulations attaching thereto shall be the responsibility of the Director General after due consultation with and in accordance with the policies and principles laid down by the Board.

11. Liabilities and duties of the Parties to the J.V.

11.1 X and Y undertake each with the other to perform and observe the matters following;

11.2 X undertakes with Y;

11.2.1 To produce all the consents and permits required pursuant to Soviet Law for the establishment of the J.V.

11.2.2 To ensure the due registration of the J.V. as required under Soviet Law and in particular due registration with the Soviet Ministry of Finance.

11.2.3 To pay and contribute all monies and other investments required under Clause 8 hereof.

11.2.4 To arrange the transport and carriage within the Soviet Union of all machinery and plant and other materials agreed to be supplied to the J.V. by Y.

11.2.5 To use its best endeavours in assisting the J.V. in purchasing leasing or otherwise acquiring all equipment tools materials raw materials transportation office and communication facilities and any other goods or matters which are reasonably necessary to implement the objectives of the J.V. and the successful undertaking of those matters specified in Clause 5 hereof and in complying with this provision X shall use its best endeavours to purchase acquire or procure all such matters at the best and most competitive prices.

11.2.6 To use its best endeavours in making available or procuring the requisite and necessary number of working telephone telefax and telex cables and lines for the benefit and use of the J.V. from its office or offices within the Soviet Union.

11.2.7 To use its best endeavours in procuring and making available to the J.V. a sufficient number of personnel to enable the J.V. to fulfil its aims and objectives and to supply full details of the age and work history and experience of each personnel member to the Board prior to their employment by the J.V.

11.2.8 To use its best endeavours in assisting Y with all applications for and procuration of all visas and permits required by law for entrance and exit and working permits from the Soviet Union in respect of all personnel to be employed by the J.V. and who are not citizens of the Soviet Union.

11.2.9 To ensure the provision of free medical health care to all personnel and employees of the J.V. excepting only the cost of any medicines utilised in providing any medical assistance or care.

11.2.10 To use its best endeavours in assisting the J.V. with a compliance in observing all customs import/export procedures, forms and applications concerning the Products, their export and import or any matter or materials utilised in the manufacture of the Products.

11.2.11 To use its best endeavours in assisting the J.V. in solving resolving or complying with any requirements of Soviet Law or of any Soviet Authority which touches upon or concerns the J.V. or the Products.

11.2.12 To use its best endeavours in affording all such assistance in promoting the J.V. in its undertaking and purpose as set out in Clause 5 above.

11.2.13 Not to enter into any agreement with any third party the purpose of which is the establishment of a joint venture in the Soviet Union or the establishment of any other legal entity or business whatsoever in any part of the world which is likely to compete directly or indirectly with the aims and objectives of the J.V. as set out in this Agreement.

11.3 Y undertakes with X:

11.3.1 To provide all capital, goods, materials, know-how, expertise and technical management and production techniques in order to assist the J.V. in undertaking and executing the Feasibility Study and for the purposes set out in Clause 5 hereof.

11.3.2 To use its best endeavours to market and fully effect sales of the Products in the internal and external markets at the best commercial prices which can reasonably be achieved for the

Products.

11.3.3 To construct erect or otherwise complete any structures or equipment which it may supply in accordance with the provisions of Clause 8 hereof.

11.3.4 To provide all technical personnel and staff that may be specified in the Feasibility Study and for the training and education of any specialist personnel to be supplied by X.

11.3.5 To use its best endeavours in assisting the J.V. with resolving or dealing with any matters which touch upon or concern the Products of the J.V. within the home state of Y.

11.3.6 Not to enter into any agreement with any third party the purpose of which is the establishment of a joint venture in the Soviet Union or the establishment of any other legal entity or business whatsoever in any part of the world which is likely to compete directly of indirectly with the aims and objectives of the J.V. as set out in this Agreement.

12. Audit and accounting regulations and requirements

12.1 The audit of the J.V. in respect of all its activities howsoever and whatsoever undertaken within the Soviet Union shall be undertaken in accordance with the law of the Soviet Union by the audit practice *Inaudit*. The style manner and form of the books of accounts of the J.V. shall be undertaken in compliance with and in due observance of the standards and codes of practice procedure and bookkeeping within the Soviet Union all which such matters shall further include and take into account the codes and practices of maintaining books of accounts within the home jurisdiction of Y and in the event that there shall be any conflict between the professional codes and practice of maintaining books of accounts within the Soviet Union and the home jurisdiction of Y then in such areas of conflict the professional codes and practices of the Soviet Union shall be deemed to apply.

12.2 The Parties shall ensure that *Inaudit* shall submit regular management accounts including the submission at three monthly intervals of a balance sheet and a profit and loss account with the necessary explanatory notes to the J.V.

12.3 The annual accounts, the quarterly balance sheets and profit and loss accounts and the management accounts shall be maintained in both the Russian and English language and all such costs in respect of the preparation of those accounts shall be the responsibility of the J.V.

12.4 The Parties agree that they shall be entitled to access at all reasonable times to the books and records of account of the J.V. and any supporting or ancillary documentation and that such inspection may be undertaken by the Parties or by their respective auditors from time to time.

12.5 The Parties agree with each other and without prejudice to the generality of the provisions of Clause 15 below that they shall not disclose or submit any financial or business information relating to the J.V. to any state or governmental authority other than of the Soviet Union or any of its state authorities.

13. Employees and staff of the J.V.

13.1 The personnel, staff and employees of the J.V. shall consist primarily of citizens of the Soviet Union but the J.V. may if it is reasonably necessary employ nationals of other countries but any such employment shall be done at the request and upon the recommendation of either of the Parties and with the further written consent of the Board.

13.2 All terms of employment with particular reference to salary, remuneration, rewards, duties, recreational, social and health benefits and social and health insurance of the employees and staff of the J.V. shall be undertaken strictly in accordance with the laws of the Soviet Union and it is further agreed and declared that the said laws relating thereto shall further apply to the conditions of employment of all foreign employees of the J.V. excepting only terms of remuneration, holidays and pensions which matters will be determined in each contract of employment for such foreign employee by agreement with the J.V.

13.3 The J.V. shall be responsible for the conclusion and observance of a collective agreement with the Soviet Union's trade union organisations which are relevant thereto and such collective agreement shall deal with and be concerned with the terms of employment of all Soviet citizens by the J.V. including the provision of all social requirements and such collective agreement shall be determined in accordance with the laws of the Soviet

Union.

13.4 In the event that the J.V. shall elect to employ any national not being a citizen of the Soviet Union such contract shall be for ____ calendar months and thereafter shall be renewed by agreement between the J.V. and the employee and it is agreed and declared that the J.V. shall be responsible to provide all such foreign employees and their families with adequate accommodation which shall include all the conveniences required by Soviet Law and Soviet custom and practice and such contract shall further require the J.V. to be responsible for the provision of medical services and health care to such employee or employees in accordance with the laws of the Soviet Union.

13.5 In order to assist the J.V. in the undertaking of its business the Parties may by agreement in writing agree that the J.V. may at its cost and expense send certain of its employees to other countries for training and qualification purposes where this is deemed desirable both in the interest of the employees and in the interest of the J.V.

14. Material-technical supply and sales and marketing of the products

14.1 In all cases where it is deemed necessary by the Parties the J.V. shall be provided with and acquire any necessary or requisite Soviet raw materials and technical resources through the purchasing services of X, and X undertakes with the J.V. to acquire all such raw materials, technical resources and other matters at prices which are the most reasonable and commercially advantageous to the J.V. and in all other cases where the J.V. is required to obtain materials, raw materials and technical resources and other matters in markets other than those within the Soviet Union then Y shall undertake with the J.V. to procure the acquisition of all such matters at the most reasonable and commercially advantageous prices to the J.V.

14.2 All sales of the products of the J.V. within the Soviet Union shall be undertaken by the J.V. with the assistance and provision of all necessary sales and marketing services available from X.

14.3 The sale of the Products in all countries other than the Soviet Union shall be undertaken by Y in the absence of any agreement between the Parties as to the sale and marketing of those Products by any other person firm or company.

15. Confidentiality
15.1 Each of the Parties agrees and undertakes each with the other that it shall not at any time during or within five years after termination of this Agreement divulge or allow to be divulged to any person any confidential information relating to the business or affairs or undertaking of the J.V. which shall include all technical and financial business and any other information relating to the J.V. and shall ensure at all times to keep such information confidential to the J.V. and the Parties thereto.

15.2 The divulgence, transmission or other passing of information relating to the affairs or undertaking or business of the J.V. may only be undertaken by agreement in writing between the Parties.

16. Insurance risks and liabilities
16.1 The property, assets, materials and all and any other goods and property of the J.V. shall at all times be insured in the full reinstatement value thereof with the USSR *Ingosstrakh*.

16.2 The J.V. shall at all times during the currency of this Agreement take out all employers liability, public liability, third party liability and occupiers liability insurance in respect of the business and undertaking of the J.V. within the Soviet Union in such sum or sums as the Parties hereto shall in writing agree to be reasonable and proper having due regard to the volume of risk entailed by the business of the J.V.

17. Force majeure
17.1 The Parties hereto agree each with the other that both Parties shall be released from their respective obligations in the event of national emergency, war, prohibitive Governmental regulation or if any other cause beyond the reasonable control of the Parties or either of them renders the performance of this agreement impossible and shall be deemed to include but shall not be

limited to earthquake, flood, fire, act of God, strike or lockout or governmental decree or order.

17.2 Upon the occurrence of any act or thing which may constitute force-majeure within the terms of Clause 17.1 above any Party seeking to rely thereon shall forthwith and in writing inform the other Party of all such circumstances and events relating to the act or event complained of and shall if required by the other Party adduce such reasonable evidence of such event, its duration and consequences and effect upon the Party relying thereon in the undertaking of its obligations and agreements contained in the J.V.

17.3 It is hereby agreed and declared that upon the occurrence of any such act or event hereinbefore described each Party shall use its best endeavours to mitigate and reduce any effect which such act or occurrence may have on the agreements, covenants and obligations of each of the Parties under the terms hereof.

17.4 In the event that any such act or occurrence as hereinbefore described shall occur each of the Parties or either of them affected by any such act or occurrence shall forthwith inform the other Party in writing of such act or occurrence and shall further inform the other Party when such act or occurrence shall no longer prohibit or interfere with the due performance and observance and compliance with the covenants agreements and conditions contained in herein and in the event that either Party shall fail to notify the other Party of such act or occurrence or the termination thereof such Party shall be liable to compensate the other Party for any losses directly attributable to the failure to make such notification.

17.5 It is hereby agreed and declared between the Parties that in the event of the happening of any such act or event hereinbefore described preventing either of the Parties from complying with their obligations contained in this Agreement, this Agreement shall be extended for such period or periods equal to such period or periods during which such Party was prevented or precluded from undertaking its covenants agreements and conditions contained in this Agreement.

17.6 In the event that any such act or occurrence hereinbefore described shall endure for a period exceeding six calendar months either Party may by notice in writing to the other forthwith terminate this Agreement without being liable for any loss or damage resulting from such termination.

18. Commencement and duration termination and consequences

18.1 This Agreement shall take effect as from the _____ day of __ _____199__.

18.2 X covenants with Y to keep it informed in writing of the progress of the application to register the J.V. with all authorities of the Soviet Union in accordance with the requirements of law and in the event that X shall be placed on notice of any difficulties in affecting such registration it shall inform Y and both of the Parties shall use their best endeavours to deal with all requisitions or other matters which may be raised by any Soviet authority in connection with the application for registration of the J.V.

18.3 In the event that the J.V. shall not be duly registered all in accordance with the requirements of the law of the Soviet Union within _____ months from the date of this Agreement then in the absence of agreement in writing by the Parties this Agreement shall forthwith be deemed to be terminated.

18.4 This Agreement shall continue for a period of _____ years and thereafter shall by agreement by the Parties in writing be continued from year to year unless terminated by 12 calendar months notice in writing given by either Party to the other and expiring at or at any time after the end of such annual periods.

18.5 The Parties hereto further agree each with the other that this Agreement may be terminated forthwith upon one Party giving written notice to the other in the following circumstances:

18.5.1 If either Party shall be in breach of any of its covenants obligations or undertakings contained in this Agreement and the other Party gives to the Party in breach notice in writing of such breach requiring it to make good the same or to remedy the same within 60 days from such notice in writing and the Party in breach fails to rectify the breach within the said period of sixty days.

18.5.2 If as a result of any governmental regulation act of state or of any governmental or state authority either Party is directly or indirectly and indefinitely limited as to its rights and duties under this Agreement.

18.5.3 In the event of any act or occurrence within the terms of Clause 17 of this Agreement for a period in excess of 6 calendar months.

18.6   In the event of the liquidation of the J.V. or in the event that either of the Parties shall unilaterally refuse to undertake its covenants obligations and undertakings herein contained this Agreement shall forthwith terminate.

18.7 If either of the Parties shall be guilty of any serious misconduct or any serious breach or non-observance of any of the conditions and obligations of this Agreement or shall neglect or fail or refuse to carry out the duties contained in this Agreement such Party shall compensate the other Party for any losses which that Party shall sustain as a result of such breach.

18.8 In this context such compensation for loss shall be deemed to include any losses sustained resulting from or attributable to production costs or expenses and any loss or damage howsoever arising to the property and goods of the J.V. and which are sustained as a result of the breach or breaches specified in clause 18.7 above.

18.9 It is agreed and declared between the Parties that all losses and loss of profit which shall not be directly attributable to the breach or breaches referred to in Clause 18.7 above shall not be treated or determined as a claim for compensation within the terms of the clause.

19. Costs and communication

19.1 Each of the Parties agrees with the other that it shall be responsible for its own costs in respect of the preparation of this Agreement but all costs incurred in respect of the registration of the J.V. shall be borne by the J.V.

19.2 All information notices and correspondence shall be deemed to have been delivered by one Party to the other if sent by registered mail or other recorded delivery system to the addresses stated in this Agreement or by agreement between the Parties hereto in writing to such other address as they may agree and that such correspondence shall simultaneously be sent by telex and telefax where such forms of communication are available at the time of delivery.

20. Arbitration

20.1 The Parties hereto agree with each other that all disputes or differences which shall at any time arise between them whether during the term of this Agreement or afterwards touching or concerning this Agreement or its construction or effect or the rights duties or liabilities of the Parties under or by virtue of it or otherwise or any other matter in any way connected with or arising out of the subject matter of this Agreement shall be determined in the first instance by negotiations between the Parties within a period of 2 calendar months from the date upon which any such dispute or difference shall have arisen.

20.2 In the event that any such dispute or difference hereinbefore referred to shall not have been determined by negotiation between the Parties within the period of two calendar months from the date on which such dispute or difference shall have arisen such dispute or difference shall be referred in writing by the Board to a single arbitrator to be agreed upon by the Parties or in default of agreement to be nominated by the President or Chair for the time being of the Chamber of Commerce of _____ ____which arbitration shall be undertaken in accordance with the laws of _____ and the decision of the arbitrator shall be final and binding upon the Parties hereto.

21. General provisions

21.1 All rights duties and liabilities contained in this Agreement are personal to the Parties hereto and shall not be assigned or be capable of assignment unless such assignment shall have first been agreed between the Parties hereto in writing and subject to the unanimous decision of the Board of the J.V. PROVIDED ALWAYS that in the event of any such approved assignment the assignee shall enter into an agreement with the Party which is not assigning any of its rights duties or liabilities under this Agreement to observe and perform and comply with the terms agreements conditions and undertakings set out in this Agreement.

21.2 Without prejudice to the generality of the provisions of Clause 21.1 above, if Y wishes to assign its rights in the J.V. it shall first offer those rights to X pursuant to article 16 of the Decree No. 49 referred to in Clause 6.1.2 of this Agreement.

21.3 The Parties declare that this Agreement constitutes the whole agreement between them and supersedes all other written or oral agreements and arrangements made between them which shall cease to be of effect as of the date hereof but the Parties may by agreement in writing agree to amend or add to the terms conditions and provisions of this Agreement provided that all such amendments and additions shall be evidenced in writing and signed by a person or persons duly authorised for and on behalf of the respective Party.

21.4 The Parties agree each with the other that while the covenants conditions restrictions and obligations herein contained are considered to be reasonable in all the circumstances it is agreed that if any such matters shall be adjudged to be void or ineffective for whatever reason but would be adjudged to be valid and effective if part of the wording thereof of the Clause thereof were deleted or reduced in scope the said matters shall apply with such modifications as may be necessary to make them valid and effective and the interpretation of this Clause shall in all respects be interpreted and determined in accordance with the laws of the Soviet Union.

21.5 The Parties now acknowledge each with the other that this Agreement shall be signed in both the English and Russian texts and acknowledge each with the other that both texts are valid in the interpretation of this Agreement.

THE ADDRESSES OF THE PARTIES HERETO FOR THE PURPOSES OF THIS AGREEMENT SHALL BE DEEMED TO BE AS FOLLOWS:-

X_____

Y_____

IN WITNESS WHEREOF THE PARTIES HAVE SIGNED
THIS AGREEMENT THIS _____ DAY OF _____
199__.

Index